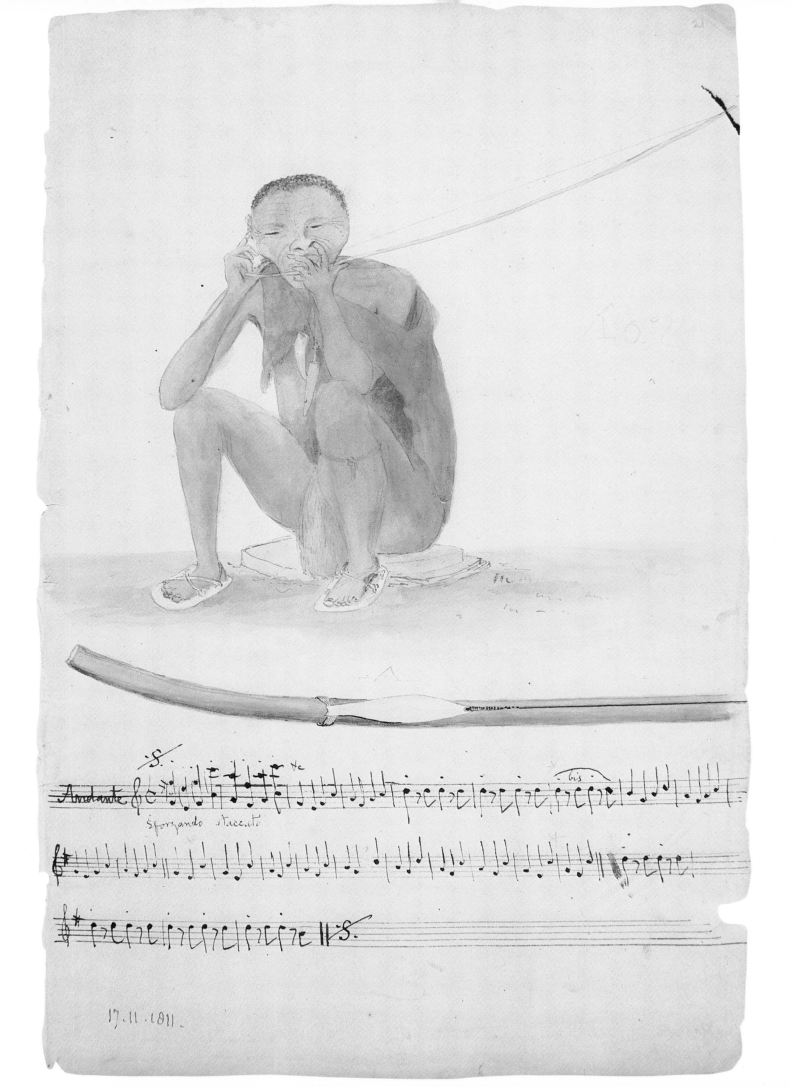

Dear A.

Last night the cattle ran away. I have no more water. I despair. I left the wagon on foot in the hope of reaching Kokong pan, but my strength fails. My private papers and stamps send to my children in _____ , and inform them that I have died of fever in the desert and am buried. As well inform B. to this effect. Charlie and the new Kalahari boy are mainly responsible for this. The thirst kills me. These are the last words of a dying man.

Your true friend
M.

P.S. A little water would have saved me.

(Letter found on the remains of a corpse that had been devoured by hyaenas and jackals, by Arnold W. Hodson, hunter-explorer, at the turn of the century.)

The ox-wagons conquered the sands of the Kalahari.

(Opposite) *Red Kalahari sand suffocates the carcass of an old traveller. Its roof has been roughly removed for a shelter elsewhere.*

THIS BOOK IS DEDICATED TO:

ALEXANDRE, ANETTE, DAVID,
JULIAN, MENDEL, SYLVIANE
AND VÉRONIQUE.

ISBN 1 86812 247 6
First edition, first impression 1989 by
Southern Book Publishers (Pty) Ltd
PO Box 548, Bergvlei 2012
Johannesburg
Originally published by Plon Publishers, France.
Set in Mallard
By Unifoto (Pty) Ltd
Printed and bound by Cronion S.A. (Barcelona)

KALAHARI
RIVERS OF SAND

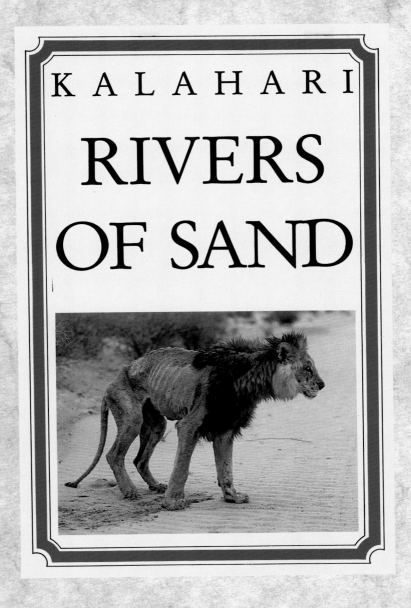

ALAIN DEGRÉ
SYLVIE ROBERT
TEXT BY MIKE KNIGHT
DESIGN BY LANCE CHERRY

SOUTHERN
BOOK PUBLISHERS

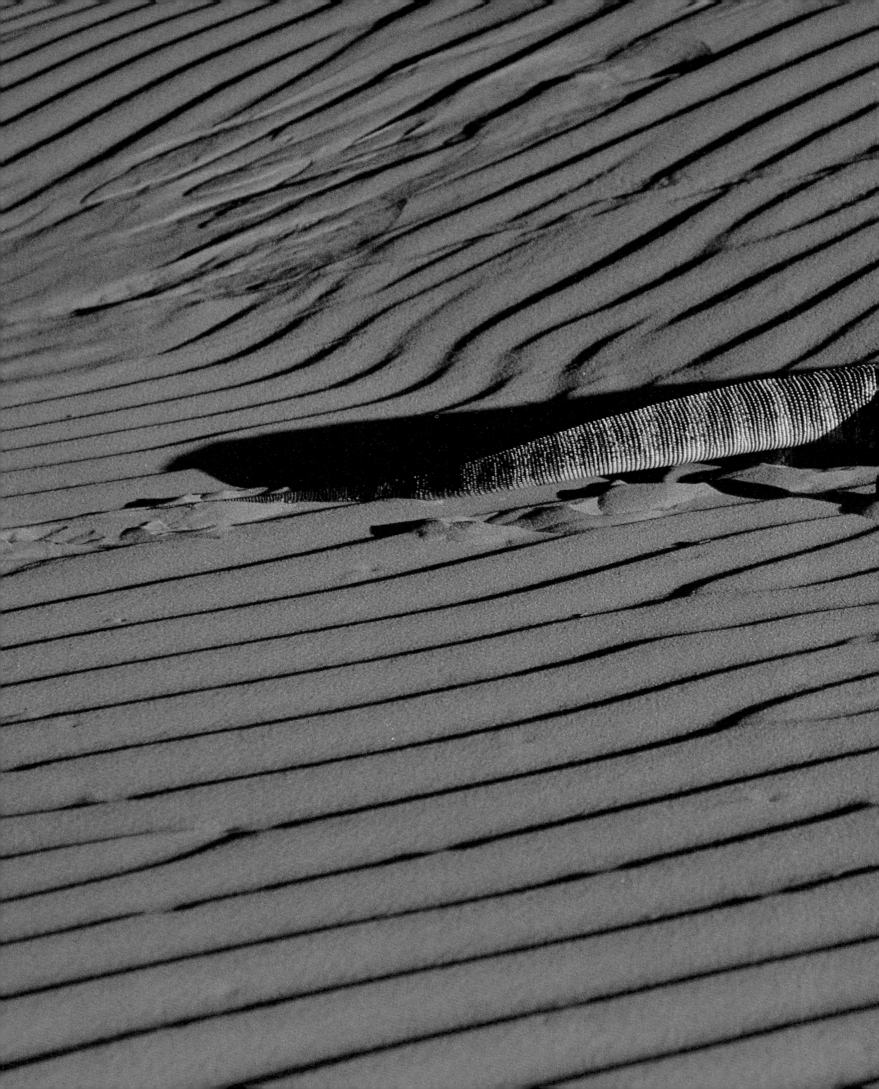

CONTENTS

Sylvie's happiness among the meerkats, the result of her five-year-long friendship with them.

(Preceding pages) A rare visitor to the southern Kalahari, the rock monitor, tastes the sand in its search for food.

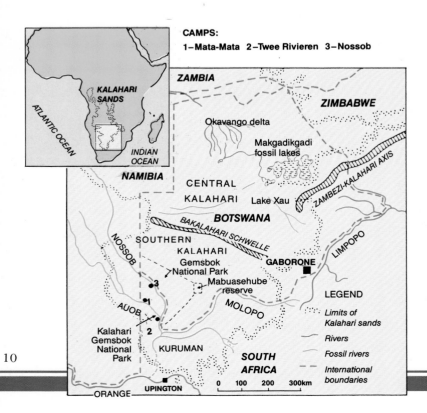

THE HEART OF THE SANDS

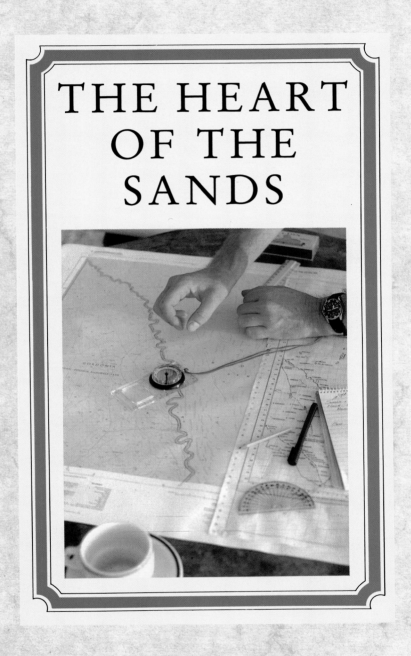

The branch crashes through the canopy of the old thorn tree, shattering the intense silence of the pre-dawn night as it hits the thick, parched trunk, before thudding onto the dry riverbed, sending up a small, billowing cloud of dust. The too heavy giant eagle owl, thrown from its fallen perch, dives into the darkness in search of a more steady resting place to continue its hungry vigil for potential prey. Silence returns to the dark pre-dawn.

With the first hint of sunrise, sparrow-weavers desert their cozy, yet precarious grass-woven nests suspended at the ends of thin *Acacia* tree branches, for perches atop the large, scattered camel-thorn *Acacia* trees silhouetted against the glowing eastern sky. Fluffed up against the cool morning air, their cheerful, noisy chirpings welcoming the dawn of another October day, still they silently pray that this day may be different from the last few.

Swooping high above in the half-light the hungry pale chanting goshawk has the only panoramic view of the area. A dark sharp horizon unmarred by any hill, mountain or river gorge; a straight line running into eternity. Casting its eyes downward, the goshawk sees the landscape begin to take form. Long dark straight shadows separated by red naked dune crests, warmly touched by the first rays of the sun, pass slowly below, one after the other in an endless succession. Isolated trees and bushes surrounded by a few tussocks of tall, dry golden grass loom out of the bare red sands as the dune shadows slowly recede. Nothing moves among the bushes or from the hundreds of small vacant holes that stare unblinkingly upwards. The line of the dunes is suddenly broken by a narrow

The beautiful Cape cobra puts up an impressive display when disturbed. The bite of an adult specimen can be fatal to humans without prompt medical attention. The venom, extremely poisonous, contains powerful neurotoxins.

vein of brown sand glistening naked in the morning half-light. It meanders slowly through the long dune shadows, making its way to the lightening horizon.

This ancient riverbed, devoid of plant growth except for the occasional large thorn tree with its thick knotted trunk and entangled mesh of branches, carries no water – only the sands of the dunes that slowly choke its course. Old, dried-up mud baths, now cracked into huge cakes of tumbled mud, lie scattered in the flat riverbed. Animal tracks permanently imprinted in the dry bed are the only reminders of the now invisible water of last summer, soon forgotten. Fresh game tracks in the dust wander down from the dunes onto the flat, lifeless surface of the riverbed in a never-ending search for a morsel to eat. The gentle melodious *wip-pi-pi-pi* of the goshawk fills the air as it abandons its search and slowly glides downward to the red inhospitable earth. Settling in the top of a large lonely tree its call joins the distant chorus of the sparrow-weavers in welcoming another day to the southern Kalahari – a land of isolation, mystery and thirst.

The Kalahari conjures up different images in the minds of different people. Some see it as a scorching desert with rolling sand dunes, the home of huge herds of nomadic antelope preyed upon by large carnivores and small bands of wandering, scantly clad Bushmen (or San, as they are more correctly known). Others see it as the mysterious domain of a long forgotten empire with lost cities buried under the once moving red sands. Yet others see it as their future, built on cattle, sheep, wildlife and those small hard stones: diamonds. The Kalahari, and particularly the more arid south, is all this but also something more: it is one of Africa's last frontiers. Inaccessibility, the continuous, unyielding red sands devoid of prominent features to steer by and, even more important, the lack of drinking water for most of the year have been barriers to exploitation, preserving it unspoilt,

The divider of the Kalahari – the fence – must be regularly checked and maintained. Dense grass stands such as "never seen before" will be plenty for the next five years . . .

(Inset) *The cast-iron sign of past colonial powers. Placed roughly 1,6 km apart along the entire border between what was then German South-West Africa and the British territories of the Cape Province and Bechuanaland Protectorate, these numbered signs were marked on maps as an aid to lost travellers.*

15

at least in large tracts of land well away from the selfish clutches of the human hand. But how long will it last?

The term Kalahari, meaning wilderness and originating from the name of the black tribe, the Kgalagadi, who occupy central Botswana, is particularly ambiguous having several interpretations. Geologically, the term refers to the upper sand layer of the Kalahari Beds. The sand particles have characteristic sizes and shapes attributable to their wind-blown or aeolian origins. This upper sand layer extends over some 2,5 million km² of the interior of central southern Africa, stretching from the Orange river in South Africa to the Zaïre river in the north, and from eastern Namibia to western Zimbabwe, thus forming the largest continuous stretch of sand in the world. The present relatively moist climates and southwestern position of the Kalahari sands in the African subcontinent, well away from direct maritime influences, account for a decreasing rainfall isocline from northeast to southwest. The highly regular average rainfall of 1 000 mm received in the Zaïrese rain forests declines to an erratic and meagre 150 mm in the northwest of the Cape Province of South Africa. Consequently the extensive Kalahari sands underlie a great variety of habitats and animal communities, adding variety to the monotonous sand.

However, the popular interpretation is that the term Kalahari refers predominantly to the more arid reaches of the sands, an area that roughly coincides with present-day Botswana. This is further subdivided into a southern and central section by an almost indistinguishable yet very important rise in the land, known as the Bakalahari Schwelle, which virtually bisects southern Botswana into two gently sloping depressions. On the northern side, the fossil river valleys of Okwa and Metatswe drain towards a huge oasis, the Okavango, in the central Kalahari. On the southern side are four ancient rivers, now predominantly dry: the Molopo, Kuruman, Nossob and Auob, all of which rise beyond the Kalahari sands. Their dry beds meander lazily southward through the dune country to a collective sandy grave just short of the ancient confluence with the Orange river.

The whole or mega-Kalahari has its origin about 65 million years ago, during what is known as the Tertiary era. This coincided with the final splitting of the super-continent of Gondwanaland, which consisted of Africa and what is now India, Madagascar, Antarctica, Australia and South America. Prior to and during the breaking apart of the continents, Africa had experienced intensely arid conditions, with mass vulcanisation and outpouring of lava, some flows being up to 9 km in depth. This was followed by further erosion, weathering and arid conditions that by 15 million years ago had reduced the mountains

Life goes on in the Kalahari.

and ridges of the African subcontinent to a huge level plain covered in moving sands. Rivers, blocked with clays and gravel and later with sand blown by strong winds, changed their courses, while depressions filled up – some to a depth of over 300 m – with the moving sands and debris of the interior. The intermittent periods of high rainfall failed to scour out the sandy deposits. The water soaked into the sands and what rivers formed, meandered and flowed slowly over the flat interior with little down-cutting force. With large-scale erosion having modified the landscape and redistributed a huge proportion of the subcontinent's mass, forces below the African continent

hari, lost its headwaters and most of its water supply and strength owing to a slight subsidence along its reaches, leaving its impressive, steep-sided gorge naked, exposed and thirsty.

Within the subcontinent's interior two important but small, barely recognisable ridges rose on the surface; they had a far-reaching impact upon the region. One of these ridges, known as the Bakalahari Schwelle, runs roughly northwest to southeast from the Namibian border near Gobabis to near Lobatse in southeast Botswana. It isolated the southern Kalahari and divided the watershed of the flat Kalahari interior about 12 million years ago. It is even suggested

A pregnant meerkat killed by an eagle.

(Opposite) *More a killer than a scavenger, the spotted hyaena survives well in the southern Kalahari. Feeding upon freshly killed carcasses, it need not drink water at all.*

are suggested to have been set in motion which resulted in twisting, warping and splitting of the continent's surface. The southern margins of Africa were tilted up and outwards, while down-warping in the interior produced at least four continuous depressions in the subcontinent. Pulling apart of the continent itself resulted in the Great Rift valley, which runs from the Sinai through East Africa and the Zambezi valley into the Okavango delta. These changes occurred relatively slowly, and some river systems maintained their ancient courses, cutting steep-sided gorges into the slowly rising rock. But the Molopo river, which cuts through the southern Kala-

that the Schwelle interrupted the flow of a huge, southward-flowing ancient river that drained the continent's interior, and redirected the river to the east where the present-day Limpopo river flows.

The other ridge, known as the Zimbabwe-Kahalari axis, begins near Gaborone and runs northwest into

central Zimbabwe. Apparently rising later than the Schwelle, it is suggested to have blocked the waters of a large east-flowing river and created, around two million years ago, a huge inland lake in the area of the present-day Makgadikgadi pans. This lake varied immensely in size over the last 50 000 years in response to the highly fluctuating climate and the slight warping of the subcontinent's surface, which redirected the Zambezi more to the east and away from the super-lake. At its fullest, when fed by the Okavango and mighty Zambezi rivers, the lake may have covered 60 000 km² and been up to 100 m deep in places. Terraced platforms created by strong wave action are in evidence around the periphery of the ancient lake, indicative of its once majestic size and nature. But today it is nothing more than a huge, wind-blown, dry salt-pan, holding scant seasonal overflow water from the Okavango delta.

The separation of Antarctica from the Australian continent ten million years ago and the subsequent weather pattern of circumpolar circulation initiated the movement and upwelling of cold Antarctic water in the form of the Benguela current flowing along the west coast of southern Africa. This had a dramatic drying effect on the Kalahari and in conjunction with the ice ages of Europe caused great fluctuations in the weather of the subcontinent, which periodically ranged from moderately wet to extremely dry. The wet periods inundated the pans of the Kalahari and supported for extended periods of time a wide variety of animal and plant life such as diatoms, crustaceans and gastropods in extensive reedbeds. The terraced edges of some pans resulted from wave action while the rivers of the Kalahari, fed almost entirely with water from beyond the Kalahari sands, flowed strongly and cut steep-sided gorges into the undulating calcrete.

The coming of more arid, hot conditions with strong winds dried up the pans and riverbeds. The drier, more desiccating atmosphere sucked the water from the sands, drawing salts to the crusty surfaces of the now white, naked salt-pans. The flow of underground water below the ancient, dry river courses continued to slowly weather and cut into the bedrock and sands, making the river gorges gradually steeper. Loosened sands from the pans, riverbeds and existing dunes in the southwestern extreme of the Kalahari were shifted and blown down-wind into a waving sea of linear sand dunes, which were subsequently stabilised with vegetation in the "wetter" present-day climate. But these dunes are again changing; they now move in some areas, not because of lack of rain, but because of man: overgrazing by his increasing numbers of livestock creates micro-deserts around the many boreholes and wells sunk in the extensive sands.

Smaller than the jackal, the Cape or silver fox hunts mainly for mice and insects. Mistakenly these foxes are hunted down as possible threats to sheep in farming areas.

The ostrich is the largest living bird, with a mass of up to 80 kg. Unable to fly, its feathers are unbarbed, loose and attractive, but form an important shield against the elements. They are highly sought after in the fashion world. Commercial ranching of ostriches for their meat, skins and feathers has become a lucrative business in southern Africa.

(Overleaf) Kalahari dunes in their natural state stretch into infinity.

"Scotty Smith" at his home in the Kalahari, with his pet ostriches and, in the doorway of the shack, three black children who were frightened by the photographer. Visitors were rare at "Scotty's" camp because he preferred to do the visiting.

Scotty Smith, alias George St Leger Gordon Lennox, a highwayman, I.D.B. (illicit diamond buyer), horse and cattle thief, farmer, soldier, mercenary, veterinarian, spy and hero, was a legendary villain of the northern Cape, whose outrageous exploits live long after him.

Of Scottish descent but raised and educated in Australia, he saw dubious service in the Indian Army before moving on to South Africa in 1880. No prison held him long — the adventure and freedom of the open bush drove him on.

After being commissioned by Lord Kitchener to spy on the Boers and later again by the Union government against the Germans in South-West Africa, he was commissioned by the Royal College of Surgeons for a more mundane task, which however turned out to be a sinister episode. He was asked to search for complete skeletons of genuine San Bushmen. This he did with fervour and without delay produced skeletons both old and fresh. Asked where he got them he said, "When I was an outlaw, the police used to send Bushman trackers after me. So I shot them. Now I'm selling their bones." It later emerged that many of the San had been neither raiders nor trackers!

Even in the present more humid period in the southern Kalahari, the single crucial factor is still water. Rainfall is restricted predominantly to the latter half of summer and ranges from an average annual total of 150 mm in the southwestern dune area to 300 mm in the northeast. Rain normally comes in the form of convective thunderstorms over the flat Kalahari sands, which deposit their crucial watery load in isolated patches, creating a mosaic of green islands of vegetation in a sea of dry, sunburnt, hungry grasses and sand. This patchiness is an important phenomenon in the southern Kalahari ecosystem, stimulating boom conditions in a few areas, while the remainder stays dry and parched, waiting for the life-giving rain. Some animals large enough to walk or fly, move to these areas to seek out their nutritious sprouting grasses, abundant seeds and flourishing faunal populations, while those unable to undertake such a journey patiently await their turn for the heavens to open upon them.

Annual rainfall varies immensely from year to year, but the total amount is less important than the spacing and size of the storms. A storm of 10 mm is considered ideal to stimulate plant growth, but should be followed shortly afterwards by another of similar size to sustain the initial growth. However, these ideal conditions are rare: over a five-year period at Nossob camp in the southern Kalahari an average of 18 rain storms occured per year, but only 15% of them delivered more than 10 mm, and they averaged 21 days apart – not particularly conducive to good plant growth!

The gradually increasing and less variable rainfall towards the northeast is reflected in the vegetation. In the rolling drier dune country in the southwestern extreme of the southern Kalahari, the dunes are thinly covered in tall waving grasses, most of which are hardy perennials. The widely spaced trees and bushes distribute themselves mainly on the dune crests and sides where the sands are deeper and the water

One of the rare tracks crossing the dunes. Sand roads usually follow the riverbeds.

(Preceding pages) The chameleon, an extraordinary animal whose general structure has remained unchanged for more than 14 million years. This "lizard" is very rarely seen today and can be considered an endangered species, mainly because of bush fires.

LEGENDARY CITY OF THE SANDS

"We camped near the foot of it, beside a long line of stone which looked like the Chinese wall after an earthquake . . . in some places buried beneath the sand, but in others fully exposed to view . . . The general outline of this wall was in the form of an arc, inside which lay at intervals of about forty feet apart a series of heaps of masonry in the shape of an oval or obtuse ellipse . . . Some of these heaps were cut out of solid rock, others were formed of more than one piece of stone, fitted together very accurately . . . On digging down nearby in the middle of the arc, we came upon a pavement about twenty feet wide, made of large stone . . . This pavement was intersected by another similar one at right angles, forming a Maltese cross, in the centre of which at some time must have stood an altar, column, or monument . . ."

So looked the city Farini found in the Kalahari sands during his 1885 expedition up the Nossob riverbed. He mentions that the ruins were located about six days' trek to the east of the Ky Ky "mountains" up the river.

Since Farini's discovery there have been no fewer than 41 attempts to locate this "lost city". None of the official expeditions ever came close to finding it during their arduous and exhausting treks into the dune seas. Infrequently, sighting reports filtered in from people who were generally on their own. They were either on illegal poaching trips and were unable to divulge their names or the ruins' location for fear of official action, or they were

lost in an aircraft over the featureless sands and could not correctly locate the ruins. Yet for others they came and disappeared in a sand storm. As late as 1986 an old lady intent on finding this mysterious ancient settlement hired an aircraft and flew to Nossob camp. One day of bumpy flying over the sands on a hot summer's day was enough to convince her that she could not find it.

Having flown over the sea of sand, I personally find it hard to believe such a city exists. Where would they have got the construction materials, wood and most important of all, water, to support such a settlement? Closer scrutiny of Farini's expedition reveals many discrepancies,

inaccuracies and even stolen bits of text from others who had written about the southern Kalahari.

Farini, born William Leonard Hunt, was an entertainer and prankster in his young days. Searching through Farini's book *Through the Kalahari Desert*, Dr A. J. Clement found many contradictions.

The 100 days in which Farini supposedly travelled the 3 000 miles (4 800 km) by ox-wagon through the Kalahari sands meant he covered 60 miles a day — an impossibility in an ox-wagon. Only 20 to 25 miles a day could be covered and then only when conditions were favourable: hard flat ground, not undulating thick sand. This throws doubt on his claims to have visited certain areas such as Ngamiland in the central Kalahari, and even the existence of a lost city.

Alain and Sylvie's main camp.

29

Cape glossy starling.

are many pans: some lie in protracted lines that span great distances, the only sign of the ancient river that once linked them, when the Kalahari flowed with water and not sand; others lie completely isolated in the flat landscape. These once important inland lakes, flooded with water and rich with reeds and animal life, are today nothing more than naked, white expanses of crusty clay and salt. They become temporary oases after summer rains, holding drinking water for short periods and attracting animal life from the surrounding dry sands to their waters and the nutritious green grasses that grow around the edges of the flat pan surfaces. Man also comes – the hunter, or the rancher with his cattle, goats and donkeys – to take all, and then move on.

However, not all of the southern Kalahari remains a huge, untamed wilderness. Land-hungry colonial powers of yesteryear sliced and resliced these dry sands, fought and shed blood over them, and now they are controlled by three separate states: Botswana, South Africa and Namibia. White and coloured or Baster settlers with their rifles, horses,

content higher. A total of eight different tree species, of which five are *Acacia* species, occur in this area, but only two remain evergreen and retain their leaves throughout the year. The others drop their leaves during the driest and most demanding late winter months.

Northeast of the dune field, the sand becomes more pink and the country gently undulating. The distant horizon becomes obscured by ever increasing numbers of trees and shrubs in sometimes dense stands of golden grass. In places the shallow, widely spreading roots of the trees and shrubs strangle the grasses in their competitive search for moisture, leaving loose, exposed sand patches that shift and ripple in strong winds. Interspersed between the wooded savannas are flat, densely grassed plains with scattered low bushes – a far cry from a desert. However, in dry years, short brown grass stubbles, hard enough to puncture a vehicle tyre, and leafless shrubs are all there is to be seen.

Looming in the distance just above the trees the remote, shimmering blue of a dune, the only prominent feature, beckons man and beast alike to the pan that lies beneath it. Adjacent to the Bakalahari Schwelle

Kgalagadi women fill empty ostrich eggs with drinking water from a small temporary pool of rainwater.

beads and brandy moved in from the south, slowly displacing the indigenous black tribes along the Orange river. Other warring black tribes with their spears and cattle moved in from the east along the dry Molopo and Kuruman riverbeds, enslaving the local tribes and forcing them to tend their cattle in the unmapped sands. Wild frontier towns such as Kuruman, Olyvenhoutsdrift (now Upington) and Tsabong arose in or around the periphery of the Kalahari sands where permanent drinking water occurred – and grew fat on the spoils of fur, feathers, skins and ivory of the lawless region. The freedom and isolation of the dunes and motionless sands seemed to rub off on the local inhabitants, stimulating a rebellious nature. Between 1800 and 1915, four separate rebellions occurred, but none came to anything. In most cases the vastness of the sands became the refuge for the fleeing rebels.

The lack of drinking water and featureless terrain in the forbidding sands to the north remained an obstacle, scaring the hardiest hunter and farmer away from entering the area, except in summer when water may be found in the rare hidden "kolks" or small muddy depressions in the fossil riverbeds and isolated pans, or scattered clusters of moisture-laden tsamma melons sometimes lie strewn over the dunes. For the most part it remained one of the last domains of the San and the basis for chilling stories told around lonely camp fires of lost, dying men and hidden cities of gold.

But that was not to remain so for long. Bore-hole

drilling machines soon began to tap the water supplies hidden deep underground. Men with sheep and goats then began to tighten their circle around the arid interior. Farms, border fences and the ever increasing number of rifles began to divide the sands into South Africa and Namibia, cutting off the indigenous game's ancient natural migration routes to the Orange river in the south. Fortunately, within Botswana the lack of finance and human pressure prevented the same exploitation and expansion into the southern Kalahari, leaving most of it totally untouched.

SANDS OF THE KALAHARI

Most of the secrets and life of the southern Kalahari are hidden below one's feet in the sands. Reaching a scorching 70°C on the surface during summer days, the sands hold life-giving water between the grains a metre or so down — a great contrast typical of the Kalahari.

The sands of the southern Kalahari display two reasonably distinct surfaces. In the extreme west and southwest the sands are piled into a belt of dunes 800 km long and 100-200 km wide, while from just east of the dry Nossob riverbed to the Bakalahari Schwelle the country is flat or slightly undulating.

Essential in the formation of the linear dunes is the presence of strong winds (above 16 km/h), a very dry climate and enough sand. The sand arises from reworking of the fine particles of the interdune sediments, further deflation of the pan surfaces and removal of alluvial deposits from the riverbeds

by the strong winds. The present dune field is thought to have developed about 19 000-16 000 years ago.

The sizes of sand grains are of extreme importance in influencing the soil's water-holding capacity. The coarser sandy soils in arid regions generally hold moisture better than finer soils because there is less run-off and thus greater penetration of rainwater. Also, the less strong capillary forces reduce upward movement of soil water, hence there is less evaporation from the soil surface. In contrast, the finer soils with their higher clay component offer poor penetration, greater run off and higher evaporation rates because of strong capil-

lary forces drawing the water to the surface.

Of the two sand types of the southern Kalahari the coarser red sandy soils cover well over 90% of the region; the finer white soils occur in the pans and riverbeds. However, the mineral and nutrient concentrations of red versus white soils are the opposite of their waterholding capacities. The pans and riverbeds are richer in minerals because their low-lying situation causes water and minerals to run into them. The downward movement of penetrating rainwater in the red sand leaches out its minerals, making it generally poorer. Hence the irony of richer soils with better quality

Donkeys, horses and camels were finally replaced with hardy motor vehicles which carried the high-powered hunting rifles deeper and deeper into the sands of Botswana in search of ever diminishing numbers of game, hunted for their dried meat or biltong and their skins. Police on camels and later in vehicles struggled to contain the rampant poaching – something had to be done to stop the carnage. The concept of a conservation area was introduced.

Initially the triangle of South African land between the then unfenced Namibian border and the two ancient Auob and Nossob riverbeds was proclaimed the Kalahari Gemsbok National Park. Over the years the adjacent Gemsbok National Park of Botswana was enlarged to link up with a reserve centred on the Mabuasehube pan complex, thus forming a conservation area, in conjunction with the adjacent Botswana Wildlife Management Areas, of 80 200 km² – one of the largest such areas in the world in which wild game are either totally protected or rationally utilised.

However, the Kalahari with its harsh, thirsty climate makes no concessions to any of its inhabitants, be they humans, sheep, gemsbok or field mice – they all experience the dust, rain and cold of this lonely, sandy wilderness, the southern Kalahari.

With the first good summer rains, leopard tortoises Geochelone pardalis emerge from their hidden retreats beneath the sands where they have hibernated through the cold winter and hot, dehydrating early summer months. Besides searching for mates, they make immediate use of the nutritious flushing grasses and succulents.

vegetation (such as on pans and riverbed fringes) nevertheless struggling for water, whereas the poorer quality vegetation on the nutrient deficient red sands has relatively easier access to water.

However, even within the red sands there is variation in colour and grain size, for example in the dunes: from the deep orchre-red sand on the loose, wind-blown crests through pink on the slopes to off-white in the inter-dune valleys or streets.

The vegetation similarly differs, with fibrous dune grasses on the crest, through the thorny wait-a-while or black thorn *Acacia mellifera* on the slopes to the three-

thorned shrubs of the streets. The crests consist predominantly of sand grains of intermediate size and no silt, while the valleys have both coarse and fine grains and the slopes something between the two. Thus the waterholding capacity increases up the slope, but the compaction and sand-burrowing conditions for rodents and reptiles improve down the slope of the dune.

Variations in sand size, waterholding capacity and mineral distribution favour different plant and animal communities, adding to the rich variety within the apparently monotonous sand of the Kalahari.

KGALAGARE
OR KALAHARI?

Place names often have an intriguing ring to them, setting one's imagination alight. This, the Kalahari does with great success, as do the other great arid regions of the world: the Gobi, Sahara, Atacama, Chihuahua and Kaokoveld.

The wonder of the Kalahari beckoned men such as Livingstone, Chapman and Selous, to name a few, who explored and hunted in the sands and tried to discover its intriguing secrets.

Famous hunter-explorers

such as Buchell and Bulpin used the words Karriharri and Kglagadi, while others such as Gordon spoke of the Macarigari to describe the sandy wilderness or thirst-land between the Orange river and the Okavango delta. The name Kalahari, as we know it today, probably originated with the famous missionary Robert Moffat, who noted that a black tribe, the Kgalagadi, came from the arid wastes to the north of Kuruman which they called the Kgalagare.

The harsh realities of colonial rule in German South-West Africa from 1884-1913.

(Preceding pages) A permanent home for chickens and people in the red sands.

THE DUST OF THE KILLING MONTH

The meerkat family surveys its territory from the security of the burrow entrance.

The rising deep red, glowing ball in the east shimmers as it ascends through the trees from its distant grave. Its colour reflects the fiery harshness of the naked Kalahari sands. Fluffed up against the motionless, cool morning air the sparrow-weavers and forktailed drongos continue noisily to welcome the sunrise with song from their elevated perches atop the scattered trees.

Most trees, having lost their blanket of leaves, look like lifeless skeletons exposing their innermost entangled secrets of brown, cracked branches and twigs. Clusters of small shrivelled orange-coloured leaves litter the sand around the parched tree trunks. Scattered tussocks of short, golden grass stand majestically erect as if to defy the surrounding loose red sands to cover them. Under the black-thorn bush, a striped mouse sifts energetically through the sand in search of grass seeds. Finding none, it moves out of view but never leaves the safety of the bush in its hungry search for food, except quickly to dash along well-worn straight paths between the bushes.

From deep within the earth, gentle murmurings emerge through a small hole in the side of a red, warmly glowing sand dune. Small clouds of dust, almost invisible, rise from within, then slowly a small head with deeply sunken black-ringed eyes peers over the burrow mouth, rapidly scanning the awakening world around and above. The single, hunched and fluffed figure is quickly joined by one, two . . . six or more other figures that form one coherent mass of fur as they huddle together, with each noisily demanding its share of the warming red rays. Within the now mesmerised bunch of meerkats, more correctly called suricates, one head begins to nod forward with closed eyes, but startles awake as it falls face down in the sand. Another, now standing more erect and us-

Granted permission to live and work, they set up home in an isolated section of the farm. "Keep my farm free of jackal is all I want, and R10,00 a skin is what I'll pay" says Mollie Moolman, the landowner.

ing its tail for support, remains constantly alert, flinging its head from side to side and upwards in a never-ending search for predators. Its hurried, short barks slam the others awake and they dive *en masse* into the too small burrow entrance. The sentry, now standing fully stretched on its hind feet, continues to bark as it stares fixedly at the homeward bound jackal pretending to be uninterested but craftily glancing towards the meerkat clan in the early-morning light.

The quietly grazing gemsbok and wildebeest bulls on the flat riverbanks suddenly raise their heads and pluck their ears in the direction of a distant lion roar that breaks the silence and reverberates through the dunes. Knowing they are safe in the warming daylight sunshine, they continue their awesome task of selecting the few remaining green grass blades. So begins an October day in the southern Kalahari.

October, the end of winter and coming of summer, heralds the beginning of hardships and endurance; the coming of strong desiccating north winds and rising temperatures that dry grasses to cinder and whip the loose sands from the dune crests – winds through which only the strongest survive. These winds, unlike the Chinook of Canada and the Sirocco of North Africa, remain nameless, arising from nowhere and going nowhere, but monumental in their influence on the environment.

Since the last rains six months earlier, the continually dry, dehydrating air and warm sand temperatures have sucked the upper sand surfaces clear of their little moisture. Plants without storage organs or with roots that do not penetrate more than a metre down into the sands wither away and die. Perennial grasses such as Lehman's lovegrass *Eragrostis lehmanniana* and the long and short-legged Bushman grasses *Stipagrostis sp.* remain dormant with their stored nutrients in their deeper penetrating roots, but

43

they keep a few active green blades in a hard, fibrous cluster of old dead leaves and stems. The roots of the perennial grasses in the upper sand layer are equally affected by the hot, dry sand and in response they have evolved a protective sand sheath around the upper 10 cm to 20 cm of their roots. In addition, they have also developed a spongy cortex in the roots which is believed to protect the central cylinder from dehydration. Surviving winter annuals, their flowers long gone, and a few remaining leaves held close to the sand surface, begin to recede with the advancing heat. Most of the large tree species, devoid of leaves, just wait, their deep penetrating roots in search of underground water. Some roots go down 50 m or more. Two thorn trees, the camel-thorn *Acacia erioloba* and the grey camel-thorn *A. haematoxylon*, as well as the shepherd's tree, *Boscia albitrunca*, retain their green leaves, forming minute oases in the sands. The cool shade of the shepherd's tree, sometimes 20°C cooler than outside, is highly sought after by all animals, from hares to lions. Besides being valuable feed the dried root bark forms a quiver and the ground roots are believed to be a cure for haemorrhoids; they also make a passible substitute for coffee or chicory. Old hollow trunks are prized landmarks for the San: they tap trapped rainwater from them.

The Parabuthus scorpion of the Buthidae family. The small pincers are indicative of a highly poisonous sting held at the tip of the arched tail. Scorpions of the family Scorpionidae, with their larger pincers, have a less potent sting and rely more on capturing and subduing their prey with their strong pincers. Meerkats and yellow mongooses, both immune to scorpion venom, are more wary of the pincers than the stinging tail.

(Preceding pages) Bathed in rain-filtered light, the springbok move slowly down the riverbed. The first rains have yet to produce green flushes of grass.

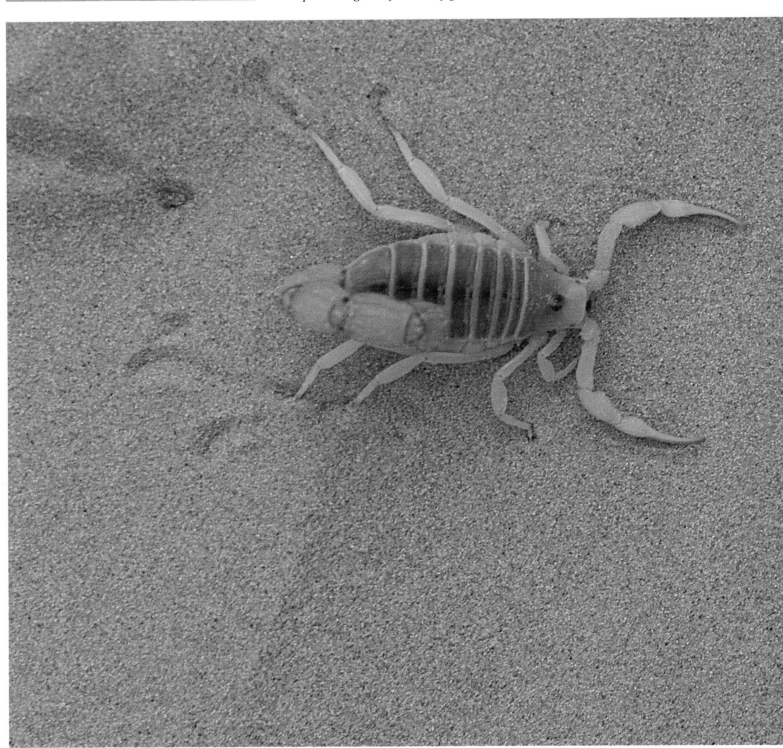

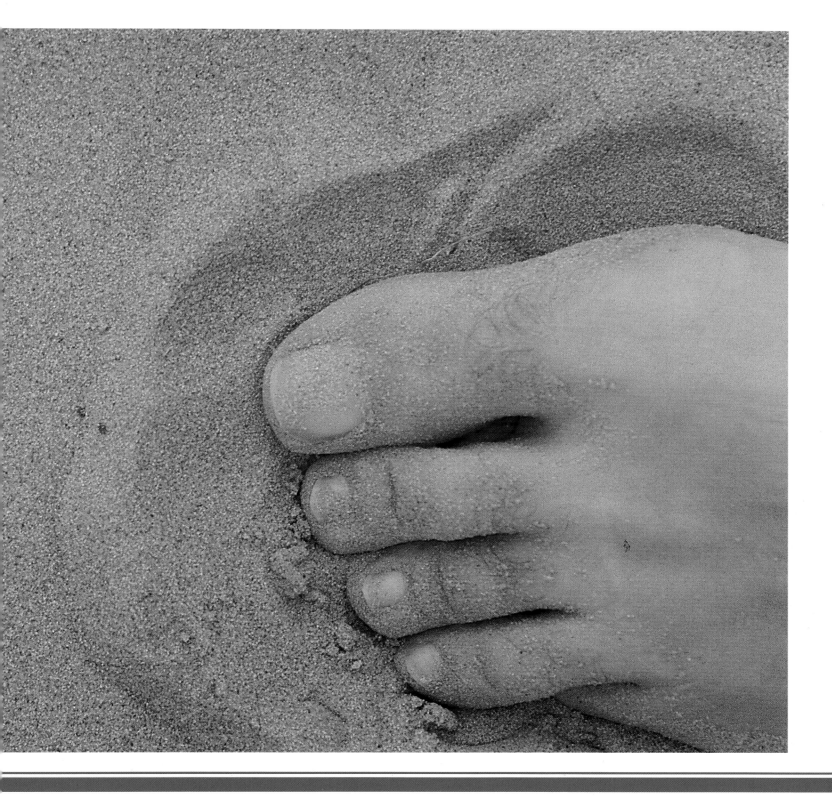

THE KALAHARI'S INHABITANTS

For almost half a million years, the Kalahari has been occupied and used by humans. During recent times the earliest inhabitants were the San. There are essentially three different groups of San: the northern, central and southern groups. The southern or Ko people occupy the southern Kalahari; where they extend into Namibia they are known as the Namas and to the south they are called Hottentots.

The San's traditional way of life was one of subsistence on nature's stores of plants and wildlife, with no necessity to grow crops or domesticate animals. They lived entirely by foraging and hunting, and are one of the few known races to have lived in harmony with nature without changing or destroying it, apart from the occasional veld fires they started. Living in small inter-related extended family bands of up to 120 people, depending on the conditions, they roamed the sands within their band's area.

Their hunting and gathering way of life does not provide the families with the means to assure their future through the accumulation of wealth. Consequently the nurturing of long-term relationships through mutual reciprocity of physical acts of giving, emotional ties and affection build a secure future or insurance policy for older age. Friction between individuals and bands is usually alleviated through accusations followed by gifts, and the expectation that the gesture will be returned one day. Even in the hunt, the animal killed belongs to the owner of the

arrow, not the one who did the killing. In this way, the whole group is involved with the hunt. On the group's return the meat is initially given to each family, who in turn gives pieces back and forth to repay debts and build bonds, so ensuring group cohesion, essential for survival in the hostile sands.

But the march of other tribes, their cultures and technologies have slowly swallowed the ways of the San, leaving no more than 2 000 individuals hunting and gathering today as their fathers did.

About 800 years ago the first groups of non-San people, the Kgalagadi, came to the eastern periphery of the Kalahari. They brought cattle and sheep, knowledge of iron, pottery and subsistence agriculture, and incorporated the San in their advance. The arrival of the Tswana in the early 1800s, also from the east, was more aggressive and resulted in the Kgalagadi being pushed deeper into the Kalahari. They progressively resorted to the San way of life to survive around the scattered pans. Further incursions by the warlike amaNdebele (a break-away Zulu group) in the 1820s pushed the Kgalagadi and Tswana collectively deeper into the sands, the San's final domain.

The records of early travellers, hunter-traders and missionaries and the oral traditions of the local peoples indicate that by the 1870s the Kgalagadi had penetrated westwards to the large pans at Tshane, Lehututu and Tsabong on the southern Kalahari periphery where permanent drinking water existed,

but that they moved further south only in the wetter months.

At the same time the push from the south by hunters and farmers was well under way, using the ancient dry Nossob and Molopo rivers as highways. The digging of wells led to permanent settlements along these rivers. By the First World War, large tracts of the Cape Province of South Africa and Namibia had been surveyed and carved up into private farmland.

These farmers, on their large pieces of land, lived incredibly hard and sometimes frustrating lives, at the mercy of the southern Kalahari. Their abodes, either piles of sticks, wattle-and-daub, or later corrugated iron houses, were humble, as they had to follow their stock after fresh water or tsammas.

Wool sheep were initially popular but the presence of sand in the wool downgraded its quality. The initial and illegal arrival of karakul sheep from Namibia in 1934 in the boot of a car set the whole of the Northern Cape economy rolling. The black pelts of newborn karakul lambs, which produce the famous astrakhan of the Middle East, found a huge market in Europe. Of late, the pressures on the natural hides and pelts industry by anti-cruelty groups in Europe and America and the more attractive mutton and beef industry, as a result of the improved road system, have drawn interest away from karakul. Relatively new sheep breeds such as the Dorper have almost replaced the traditional Merinos in the Kalahari.

San family.

George Mennie, owner of 40 000 ha near Mata-Mata in Namibia, counts his sheep.

For 52 farmers of the central salt block of the northern Cape Province, where not a drop of fresh borehole water is to be found, expensive but welcome Orange river water is pumped from 200 km to the south.

Land prices have risen sharply in the last 80 years. Realising the Kalahari's potential the South African government spent R12-R14 million on laying a 200 km pipeline from the Orange river to a group of 52 farms north of Upington that had no fresh borehole water. However, the Kalahari's last weapon remains its unpredictable rain: alternating periods of relentless drought, followed by good years, demand caution and conservatism in restrictive farming practices. Stocking rates of 1 sheep to 6 ha and one cow to 20-40 ha must be continually varied, depending on the veld conditions.

Within Botswana's southern Kalahari, the present system of unmanaged, free wandering and often too large herds of cattle and sheep around limited watering points needs to be changed. A possible system of frequently rotating herds between watering points would reduce the veld deterioration characteristic of the many cattle posts in the Kalahari sands. But above all, diversifying the economy should be pursued. In a region without any known mineral potential, with a poor road system and lack of water, emphasis should be placed on that renewable resource that needs comparatively little investment: the game. With a rational, well-controlled utilisation programme combining tourism, hunting and the industries associated with it, the southern Kalahari has great potential for Botswana. Through this approach large tracts of untouched land can be maintained, the overflowing populations can be accommodated in the hunting industry and the old, wild and mysterious southern Kalahari with its herds of antelope can be preserved for us, our children and the world.

Much the same way as grasses protect themselves from grazing with toughened fibrous stems, so these evergreen trees have foul-tasting tannins and phenols to deter browsing. However, a delicate balance is necessary as these chemicals or secondary compounds are expensive for the plant to manufacture and too high concentrations reduce the tree's ability to capture the sun's energy, or photosynthesise, and manufacture food. Browsing on its leaves by steenbok, springbok, eland, goats and even insects stimulates the production of higher levels of these chemicals within the tree. If ingested in large quantities the chemicals are detrimental to the browsing animals' rumen and gut flora by binding up the released proteins and hence denying them to the host, which then essentially starves to death with a full stomach. For this reason the ungulates mix their diets as much as possible, taking small portions from the different species and individual trees and even from different areas, as the trees are able to communicate locally between each other about the browsing pressure on them from animals.

As a welcome temporary relief to the hungry ungulates and an ideal opportunity for cross-pollination some species such as the black thorn, grey camelthorn and shepherd's trees draw upon their food reserves and gingerly produce their dense clusters of sweet and sometimes heavily scented blossoms. In places the dune sides, brown with dirty naked bushes on lifeless red sands, are transformed into yellow patches of colour; the flowers quickly fade, drop and fall to the ground, their job done.

The standing grass and thin, vulnerable tree twigs begin gently to waver as the warming early-morning air stirs. Birds flutter among the bushes searching for seed patches and insects, grazing gemsbok continue to feed while the now recovered suricates leave the burrow on their morning foraging trip towards the fossil riverbed. Dead *Acacia* blossoms begin drifting across the open sands, collecting in small heaps in vacant whistling burrow entrances and track depressions left by a passing gemsbok bull on his territorial patrol. The fine dust kicked up by the hooves of a herd of springbok gently drifts away from them as they cross the dry, glistening riverbed.

The air becomes warmer as the stronger wind caresses the heat from the sands. Gusts begin to whistle through the now moving branches. Sand grains begin to roll down the slip faces of the dunes. Sheets of dust are raised from the riverbed, temporarily obscuring the scattered camel-thorn trees that eerily loom out of the hot suffocating blanket, which enfolds animals and traps the radiating heat from the ground. Above, the hazy sphere of the sun continues

The unblinking stare of a Cape vulture, previously plentiful birds that are now close to extinction.

(Overleaf) *Motionless and hidden, a springbok lamb attempts to escape detection, but many fail.*

The first ray of the early morning sun warms the cold-blooded ground dwelling gecko, a delicacy for meerkats.

to pour its energy on the now dust-covered riverbed, making the heat even more oppressive. Streaky beams of sunlight that break through the dust clouds dance on the minute pieces of formica floating in the clay dust. Over the sound of the wind, unseen, a lost springbok lamb softly bleats its desperate cry for its mother, who fixedly stands well away with other springbok. Her head held low and back to the wind, she patiently waits out the dust storm.

Beaten back by the flying sand that pierces their fur like pins and blocks their eyes, the suricate family hesitantly move back towards a burrow on the now distant riverbank. Frequently stopping, they all stand clustered closely together, peering out into the hazy, choking void, not knowing exactly which way to go. The one baby moves nervously between the standing adults' legs, aware of the apprehension among the group but ignorant of the possible sources of danger. Their constant soft mutterings help build up their confidence to move on again. With heads held forward and tails erect as sticks the uncertain group charges *en masse* into the hazy, suffocating world. The burrow they finally find has to be shared with two ground squirrels, also cowering from the barrage of sand and dust.

From far off in the dunes, the billowing clouds of brown dust that are thrown high into the seemingly tranquil blue sky follow the meandering riverbed to the southeast. Constant sheets of sand stream from the dune crest down the steep slip face and progressively swallow the small three-thorned bushes at the base. In the open, game tracks and rodent holes disappear under the now rippled sand surface. Lying on the down-wind side of low black-thorn bushes gemsbok and steenbok alike escape the lashing wind and sand, but not the burning sun. Birds, large and small, precariously clutch the shaking branches deep within the more protected canopies of the trees and bushes. People likewise retreat to the inner sanctuaries of their homes or grass huts while their sheep, exposed to the elements, hang their heads and cluster together in groups.

Everything seeks shelter and protection; the wind has won yet again. Later it will be the sun and heat . . .

The black mane of a Kalahari lion is flattened and splayed to one side of his thick neck by the wind. He peers through the dust and leafless black-thorn bush at the lone hazy-grey figure standing on the dune side. His orange eyes and contracted pupils concentrate on the target ahead. To the right, the lioness moves slowly, dragging her belly on the ground, head outstretched and black tail tip nervously twitching. The grey-and-white gemsbok bull raises his head, the thick, long horns rapier sharp. The lioness stops in mid-stride and slowly subsides to the ground, never taking her unblinking eyes off the bull, ten metres away. As the gemsbok again lowers his head to sniff the ground, the two predators move quickly forward, making sure each paw touches soft soundless sand. Raising his head again, the gemsbok casually looks around the wind-blown, dusty landscape, unaware of the impending danger. Again the two lions drop down and flatten themselves on the sand; they shift their paws gingerly under their trembling bodies. The needle-sharp horns of the gemsbok dip down again. The lion gives a short grunt as he bounds three metres forward. Startled, the gemsbok instinctively recoils from the sound and charges between two black-thorn bushes. From behind waving grass on the dune crest a second lioness bursts down the slip face to steer the fleeing gemsbok back to the left. Tearing round the side of the thorny bush, the gemsbok flashes his horns at the blurry image leaping towards him. On turning to the right, his hind legs suddenly collapse under the mass of the lioness as she desperately digs her claws into the straining gemsbok's thick, muscular haunches. His one horn penetrates flesh as he violently stabs them backwards in one powerful movement. Freed of the wounded lioness, he only just manages to stand before the huge lion clasps his paws around the bull's neck and sinks his crushing teeth into the muscle. Pouncing with force onto the bull's exposed back, the other lioness knocks the entwined gemsbok and lion to the ground. The guttural roar of the bull and his thrashing legs that send curtains of sand raining into the turbulent air fail to throw the predators from him. The lion's deeper clenching canines sever the gemsbok's jugular, sending a fountain of dark hot blood spurting to the sand. His twisting body and now gurgled moans grow weaker as the Kalahari begins to fade from view through his bulging, unblinking eyes. Life gone, the two lions release their limp prey and collapse, panting from the extreme exertion.

Lying to one side, the second lioness breathes in gasps as blood oozes from her punctured lung. She won't survive to eat the fruits of her last kill.

A rare encounter with a wild cat, as it quietly waits above a rodent hole.

(Opposite) *A few days before her babies' birth, Cicatrice smiles proudly. She is the "mamma" of the group that Alain and Sylvie followed for five years.*

Recovered, the large male straddles the hard-won prize, clasps it by the neck and effortlessly drags it to the nearest shade of a small camelthorn tree. Then the feast begins: they tear at the warm flesh to get at the nutritious heart and liver. Soft cat-like calls drift down from the dune as three small cubs slip and slide their way down the loose slip face towards the gemsbok. Cautiously, they approach the feeding adults only to be scolded and sent scurrying away. They will have to wait their turn – last.

Lying in the shade of nearby bushes, the black-backed jackals eagerly watch the pride's activities, knowing their turn will also come to scavenge from what is left of the gemsbok, that is if their rivals, the hyaenas and vultures, fail to arrive.

The driving wind, dust and now heat drive the animals deeper into their shaded and protected shelters. Through noonday and early afternoon the storm continues, never abating. As the light begins to fade, the dust gradually settles and the wind dies to a gentle breeze leaving a hushed, changed world. In the soft red light of the now setting sun plants no longer look green but off-brown with their layer of fine clay. The scattered trees, bushes and buckled grasses stand out from the clean swept sands, blown into miniature rippling dunes. Stiff gemsbok and spring-bok rise from their hiding places, stretch and begin their delayed feeding session. Dusty jackals shake their pelts and eye the gemsbok remains with renewed interest. Below the brandy-bush *Grewia flava*, the sand suddenly begins to subside, then spray out in a small stream as a whistling rat goes about the arduous task of clearing out its many blocked burrow entrances. Bird calls again slowly begin to waft through the dunes.

The strong wind, dust and daily rising temperatures make every animal's search for the rarest commodity, water, even more critical. Plants and animals alike are at their lowest ebb during the early summer months, conserving their water reserves as best they can. Grass moisture content drops to a low 2% in October, too low to satisfy the water demands of grazing ungulates. They have to resort to other sources of water, such as tsamma melons or makatane *Citrullus lanatus*. These volley-ball sized fruits, initially green but fading to yellow, with their rather tasteless watery insides, form a very important substitute for drinking water. But their distribution and numbers are so dependent upon the right rainfall that in some areas and even years there is none but in others dense stands of them litter the dunes. An illustration of how greedily the game consume them when available is that of a population of melons I monitored in the dunes, which in June averaged one melon per square metre over nine hectares (i.e. a total of 90 000 melons) not one melon was left by October of the same year. Regular low-level flights over the South African and Botswana Gemsbok National Parks revealed that even with the reasonably good rains received during that summer, only a few areas had good tsamma mel-on numbers. The Botswana section appeared to have hardly any. Insects, rodents, birds, antelope and the large carnivores all make extensive use of them, as do farmers who drive their cattle and sheep into areas where they occur but where no drinking water exists. The large antelope such as gemsbok, unable to bite open the melons, clench them between lower incisors and dental pad and shake their heads vigorously, which breaks the melon's hard outer rind. They never consume the whole melon but leave pieces strewn over the sand – a feast for insects and birds. Rodents are also important in opening up the melons; they gnaw small holes through the rind, giving otherwise helpless insects and birds access to this important resource. Brown hyaenas, with their wide-opening mouths, easily bite open the melons; they also carry them whole back to their dens for their cubs to use.

Another important aspect about the consumption of tsamma melons is that through the faeces of antelope and carnivores the tsamma seeds are spread far and wide. The acid stomachs of these animals reduce the hard, protective outer coating or testa of the seed, which facilitates germination with the coming of good rains. The rodents and insects, on the other hand, not only eat the watery flesh of the melons, but also bite into the seeds for their important fat and protein stores, destroying them completely.

Many of the early explorers of the Kalahari relied entirely upon the tsammas for themselves and their transport animals. The notorious G.A. Farini, otherwise known as William Leonard Hunt, who started the mystery of a lost city in the Kalahari, mentioned that for days on end they relied on tsamma melons for water. Having "enjoyed" them boiled, fried and the juices mixed with coffee he did not mind if he never saw another again. Hodson, an earlier explorer, found tsamma juice mixed with cocoa quite acceptable. Joep le Riche and Gert Mouton who regularly patrolled the newly proclaimed Kalahari Gemsbok National Park actively sought out patches of tsamma melons when they trekked into the rolling dunes with a cart pulled by six donkeys. Their later use of camels was a welcome relief: camels can go for seven days without drinking water.

The South African and Bechuanaland Protectorate police forces also used camels extensively from about 1914 to the 1950s on their wide-ranging patrols. The drinking troughs, old kraals and camel store, signs of the once huge breeding farm at Witdraai police station, are still evident today in the Kuruman riverbed. Stories of the problems in teaching the camels to carry riders and packs still float around among the old people of the area. In honour of this important animal a life-size bronze camel and rider statue has been erected in Upington.

The three-week-old babies come out of the burrow for the first time. The two baby-sitters are on the alert.

Vet Piet the tracker.

"The morning was cool as we started plotting our flight path for the first Kalahari balloon flight, the sun still hiding behind the dunes ...
Every 15 minutes we set off a small helium-filled balloon and watched its direction carefully until it faded into the dawn.

At last, we had plotted a course we were sure would be safe enough to attempt on our first flight. The wind was mild, blowing from the west at about 5 km/h. It was already getting light by the time we left our camp; the sky was clear except for some cloud in the west, but it did not look like anything to worry about.

By the time we reached our launch site, 2 km east of the Auob river and 20 km from

Julian, Mike Knight's son, has lived his whole life in the Kalahari.

Twee Rivieren, the sky had become overcast and the temperature had risen to 18°C, but the wind was still friendly, so we began preparations to launch our balloon: 30 minutes later we were airborne, climbing slowly at 30 m per minute. As we ascended above the sand dunes we drank in a spectacle that words seem inadequate to describe: it was like a vision of eternity, a beautiful, untouched, unspoilt, harsh yet spectacular Garden of Eden ... countless kilometres of dunes covered by small scrubby bush and patches of bright desert flowers, every colour of the rainbow, spread out in perfect harmony.

We were speechless for a long time, each experiencing the emotion of this new dimension in our own way, and not wanting to talk in case it was all a dream.

Eventually, the crack of the balloon burners suddenly brought us back to reality and we noticed the sky around us becoming darker and the air growing colder. We were now at 600 m above ground level, still on course, but the Nossob river lay 5 km away and I was having doubts about making it to the river before the storm hit us. But we flew on, Alain taking every opportunity to film the wonderful scenery. We had learnt a lot about the weather in the Kalahari and the speed with which it changes. We realised that should we be blown off course, the chances of being found in a hurry would be

THE ILLUSTRATED LONDON NEWS

REGISTERED AT THE GENERAL POST-OFFICE FOR TRANSMISSION ABROAD.

No. 2409.—VOL. LXXXVI. SATURDAY, JUNE 20, 1885. WITH SUPPLEMENT AND COLOURED PICTURE · SIXPENCE. By Post, 6½d.

very slim. We had not thought of taking along a tracking device, but our radios offered some consolation and we were able to give our ground crew (Sylvie and Vet Piet) a fairly accurate position.

We were now approaching the Nossob river and it was time to prepare for landing. We were still enchanted and did not want to end this dream, but we were about to be hit by the storm and there was only one decision to make, LAND!

We descended at 200 m per minute and levelled off above the trees that lined the riverbed; the wind had not yet gained velocity and we touched down gently in the riverbed. Moments after we landed the heavens opened and the wind blew with force, dragging the balloon through the river and leaving us halfway up a sand dune – but we were safe!"

MARTY DE KOCK
HOT AIR BALLOON PILOT

The San, like the animals who have access to rainwater for only a few months of the year, rely almost entirely upon plants, notably the tsammas, for their drinking water. Good tsamma crops are enough to make these simple people ecstatic. (A city dweller placed in a similar position, without baths and running water, would become thoroughly depressed.) Buried in the sand the melons store very well, and remain edible for up to two years. The San also make use of the nutritious seeds, crushing them into a fine powder which when mixed with water makes a tasteless but healthy porridge.

Two other melons also occur but they are smaller and less common. The wild cucumber *Cucumis africanus* and gemsbok cucumber *Acanthosicyos naûdinianus*, both of which can be bitter in certain areas, are also eaten by humans and animals. Both are covered in rows of fine, fleshy spines that act as limited deterrents to their being eaten. The local San plunge a small stick into the cucumber to test if it is bitter or rotten before they eat any.

Even where there are no melons or cucumbers, there is yet another source of moisture, but this is only available to those species that dig for it. The enlarged tap root of the gemsbok cucumber penetrates down about 1,5 m into the sand. Steenbok, springbok,

The dense stands of green grass completely obscure the red sands of the rolling dunes in years of good rain.

gemsbok, hartebeest and eland all excavate and chew the highly fibrous watery pith for its bitter, yet life-saving moisture. Wildebeest are exclusively grazers throughout the year; they never dig for the tap root. Maybe they are not as efficient as the other species in smelling out the large tap roots. As part of my introduction to the Kalahari soon after my arrival my San tracker produced a small cutting of this nourishing looking food item, saying that it quenched one's thirst on hot days. One taste was all that was needed to make me spit the morsel out, which amused the keen onlooker no end for the rest of the day: he knew full well that the bitter taste lingers on for quite a while.

Tsamma melons and gemsbok cucumbers, Acanthosicyos naudinianus, source of water for gemsbok, hartebeest, eland and humans during the dry winter.

(Inset) *During the 1985 drought the dry atmosphere hardened the skin of carcasses, so preserving the victim's last struggling posture.*

(**Overleaf**) *The hardships of the early days in the Kalahari are written into Gert Mouton's face and smiling eyes. He has been employed as a ranger since 1934 alongside Joep le Riche, the Warden of the Kalahari Gemsbok National Park. These two men have seen the area transformed from a harsh poacher's paradise into a well-organised and world famous game sanctuary. Beginning with a donkey cart, then camels and now a four-wheel-drive pick-up truck, they have been patrolling the thirst-land to enforce the Park's regulations.*

THE GAME REFUGES AND THEIR WARDENS

Diminishing game numbers in the face of increasing penetration into the sands by poachers and farmers instigated the creation in 1931 of the Kalahari Gemsbok National Park between the Nossob and Auob riverbeds. Botswana (then the Bechuanaland Protectorate) responded a few years later by creating a national reserve 40 km wide down the length of the eastern Nossob riverbank. Jurisdiction over this isolated park was given to the adjacent South African rangers as Botswana lacked the finances and logistical means to manage the park. Further extended in 1972 to the east to adjoin the Mabuasehube Game Reserve, this complex, together with the surrounding Wildlife Management Areas, is one of the largest conservation areas in the world.

Law enforcement in this huge area of inhospitable terrain has proved a challenging and often disheartening task for the Le Riche family, who for over 60 years through unceasing drought, freak floods and the unrelenting African sun have guided the development of this area. Heavy rains and the first floods in a century brought malaria, which caused the death of Johannes le Riche, the first ranger, in 1934. His successor and brother, Joep le Riche, and his single assistant, Gert Mouton, from their humble "hartbeeshuisies" (wattle-and-daub houses) patrolled the newly proclaimed and undemarcated boundaries, initially on horseback, then on camel and much later in a four-wheel-drive vehicle. A patrol of over 650 km up and down the Nossob by camel,

with water to be found in only four places — two of which were 250 km apart, was nerve-racking: the rangers' survival depended upon their transport animals.

Proclamation of the adjoining Gemsbok National Park in Botswana meant relocating a few small native settlements along the Nossob river, whose inhabitants eked out a living from cattle, hunting and the illegal trade of skins and biltong. This removed a poaching problem from the overburdened Joep le Riche. In fact the very day the park was proclaimed he arrested a party of local poachers with 56 ostrich and 60 jackal hides. But people

caught in those years were not necessarily peasant farmers, but also affluent people from far afield and even some friends who farmed locally. The pilgrimage to church every Sunday often revealed who was away on illegal hunting trips!

The increase in poaching after the end of the Second World War, owing to the extraordinary abundance of weapons and ammunition, began to take its toll on the wildlife. In one week Joep le Riche apprehended 42 poachers who had killed 45 head of big game and many more smaller species. The Bechuanaland Police in Tsabong were officially ap-

proached to help. This resulted in an excellent working relationship which exists even today.

Fences were erected along the southern and western borders of the South African Kalahari Gemsbok National Park from 1958 to 1966, to stop the indiscriminate shooting of game on the neighbouring farms. The fence was later extended north along the Botswana-Namibia border and along the Molopo river in the south, finally blocking the access of the migratory springbok, wildebeest and eland to the Orange river in the distant south. But within Botswana, the southern Kalahari remained open, free and unfenced.

With the creation of two ranger posts in the Kalahari Gemsbok National Park, filled by Joep's two sons Stoffel and Elias, the workload was lightened for the now ageing Joep. The extreme isolation, hardship and meagre salary of £6 to £7 per month for the first rangers required utmost dedication from these men and their wives. Even today the four-hour drive by vehicle to the closest town Upington, a far cry from the two-week journey by horse and cart of 50 years ago, seems too long and strenuous for most folk.

Today, the South African Kalahari Gemsbok National Park, with its three rest camps at Twee Rivieren, Mata-Mata and Nossob, provides excellent opportunities for tourists to delve into the beauty and harshness of the southern Kalahari. The Botswana section remains undeveloped except for a recently constructed ranger's post near Twee Rivieren.

The lack of surface drinking water for most of the year used to be a feature of the Kalahari sands, the "land of great thirst". Now permanent pools of borehole-fed drinking water are available year-round in the Kalahari Gemsbok National Park, but not in the adjacent Botswana park. As most of the borehole water emanates from ancient or fossil aquifers, the vast majority of drinking holes provide saline or mineralised water. Borehole depths in the region range from 40 m to 120 m.

During the severe drought of 1985, which affected the whole of the southern hemisphere, there were areas in the southern Kalahari where the gemsbok had excavated so many gemsbok cucumber tubers that it was virtually impossible to drive through there with a four-wheel-drive vehicle. Most of the dune streets looked like mine-fields – which accounted for one of my vehicle's leaf springs cracking. The tubers were not totally eaten up and once covered with the shifting sand, they grew again.

Animals such as the subterranean common mole-rat *Cryptomys hottentotus*, which live in colonies of up to 12 individuals, are totally dependent on the gemsbok cucumber for their very existence in the red Kalahari sands. Like the antelope they never completely consume them but only take relatively small samples. Sometimes they eat away a spiral-shaped section on the outside of the cucumber, like the bannister of a spiral staircase. Total destruction of their food source would necessitate moving to another area, which for these small underground-living creatures is practically impossible. The large antelope, however, can easily move to other areas.

In the absence of tsamma melons, the San also resort to sucking the fibrous gemsbok cucumber root for water, but for the unaccustomed stomach this leads to nausea and diarrhoea. Freddie MacDonald, commonly known as Kalahari Mac, by profession a

The entangled branches of the most common tree in the southern Kalahari, the camel-thorn *Acacia erioloba*. Camel-thorns provide food in the form of leaves, flowers and pods; shelter for birds, lizards and tree rats, and stabilise the shifting sands.

notorious lion hunter in the Kalahari in the early 1900s, tells how he was once saved from dying of thirst by sucking the bitter cucumber, a practice he saw during his many encounters with the roving clans of San. His thorough observations of the San's way of life often paid off during his years of wandering through the Kalahari sands. However, in very dry years even the San become desperate. Once the stores of tsamma melons and ostrich eggs filled with water are exhausted and there are no dried-out runners of the cucumber – tell-tale signs of where the tap roots occur – the San struggle to survive and many die, sometimes whole clans. Freddie MacDonald mentions that during droughts the normally very shy San would actively seek him out and ask for water. Gert Mouton remembers that on a camel patrol during the 1936 drought, near the dry Seven Pans in the Kalahari Gemsbok National Park, he and Joep le Riche came across a group of 20 San desperate for water. Having given them water and food, the rangers encouraged them to return to their headquarters in the south of the Park, which gave rise to the permanent San presence in the Park. It was the express concern of Minister Piet Grobler, instrumental in proclaiming the Kalahari Gemsbok National Park, that the game refuge should also be a haven for the rapidly decreasing numbers of San tribesmen. This group of San formed a small settlement in the southern section of the Park from which they hunted as before. However, with their extended family units and social practice of repaying debts with favours the settlement grew too big and had to be dismantled. These San were integrated into the Park personnel, where many of the descendants of the original group still work.

For some people the Kalahari has brought only unhappiness and tragedy. A letter found on a white man who died trekking with his wagon and cattle between Lehututu and Kokong pans in Botswana evidences the agony he experienced (see p.4).

Stories of lush grazing and a freer country in the northwestern Kalahari filtered through to discontented farmers in the newly proclaimed Transvaal Republic. Unhappy with new laws and regulations in the Transvaal, they started the tragic Dorsland (Thirstland) Trek through the Kalahari. Gert Alberts, Lourens du Plessis and Jacobus Botha led a total of 600 Boer farmers in 186 ox-wagons. These farmers decided to resort to the typical Afrikaner solution to discontent – they trekked.

The first breath of life for a springbok lamb. Labour can range from 20 minutes to four hours, and during this period the mother and her lamb are particularly prone to predation. Once born, the lamb is licked clean and left alone in the grass while the mother wanders off to graze.
(Opposite) *After a day's feeding on caterpillars and grasshoppers along the riverbed, Abdim's storks roost alongside rainwater pools in the Nossob riverbed, also a welcome escape from scorching summer heat for a spotted hyaena.*

Tabula noua partis Africæ.

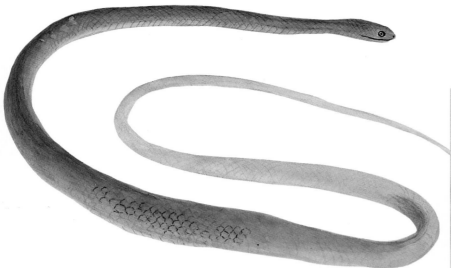

(Opposite bottom) *"Smasher hats turned up on one side, tight khaki tunics, bandoliers, white riding breeches, blue puttees and black shining boots with spurs" was the uniform of the Cape Mounted Police of the northern frontier. Camels formed the backbone of the border patrols until 1951 when the remaining 121 police camels where auctioned off at Witdraai camel breeding station in the Kuruman riverbed.*

Three separate treks in fact took place. The first was small: 12 families in 50 wagons led by Gert Alberts in 1875 crossed the thirsty sands to Ghanzi and Rietfontein, and did so without any mishap or loss of human life.

The second trek, led two years later, in 1877, by Lourens du Plessis, was much larger and consisted of 480 people in 128 wagons with many head of cattle. Moving in such a large group over terrain not capable of carrying masses of stock and people meant that existing food and water supplies were totally inadequate. The many cattle turned the limited pan waters into quagmires, unfit for human consumption.

Thirst took its toll on cattle and people alike during the slow, hard progress through the heavy sand. A total of 37 people died and a fifth of the wagons with their furniture and implements were abandoned during the first 260 km to the Boteti river in the central Kalahari; hundreds of cattle perished of thirst. In some instances the desperate trekkers shot game for the foul-smelling rumen water, their only source of drinking water: tsammas were scarce.

The third and smallest trek of 40 people in eight wagons under Jacobus Botha experienced no problems as they were moving in smaller numbers. By 1881, when the remaining trekkers reached the Humpata plateau in southern Angola, the pitiless Kalahari sands had taken a toll of over 200 people. It was an experience none of the survivors wanted to repeat . . .

Sometimes humidity reaches dew point: the air becomes 100% saturated and water condenses in the form of dew. This is, however, rare in the Kalahari, occurring only a few mornings after summer rains and

(Above) *The bad reputation of hyaenas is not justified. Living close to them reveals them to be very attractive.*
(Page 72) *Fifty years a missionary in the field, Dr Robert Moffat, with his wife Mary, laboured among the Batswana people at Kuruman on the southern edge of the Kalahari sands. The equally famous Dr David Livingstone, who married one of the Moffats' daughters, also called Mary, in the same tradition extended the frontiers beyond the great Zambezi river to the north.*
(Page 73) *Among the pioneers of the Kalahari are the Basters (Afrikaans for half-breed), as they call themselves with pride to this day. For generations they have held onto their white traditions and ancestry. At the end of the last century, pressure from white farmers coming from the south forced the Basters to move deeper into the Kalahari, where they established their own republic of Mier.*
(Preceding pages) *Kwang pan, a dry and sunbaked dust bowl, is in fact a fossil lake.*
(Page 75 inset) *The mysterious and unknown African interior in 1552.*

MEERKAT VALLEY REVISITED

At the sand crater they stand, close together, in the soft early-morning light, the remaining heroes — Cicatrice, Ugly, two bachelors and seven subadults — the last remnants of meerkat valley. United they are a pillar of strength, alone and separated they wither away into the sands. Looking anxiously into the flat, desolate and distant horizon, the thought makes Cicatrice, the matriarch and leader of the small band of meerkats, shiver and snuggle closer to her neighbour. Between them and the rising sun stand many small bushes, tussocks of golden, dry grass, several towering parched trees and the dry dusty riverbed — their valley, territory and home.

Only Cicatrice and her old faithful, loving mate Ugly have seen many such sunrises in this valley from these holes. A few seasons before there were only bushes and trees, no grass, and driving waves of naked sand. Those were hard times. The rains had failed and food was scarce. No one did sentry duty then as they all had to dig long and deep for the meagre beetle larvae and foul-tasting millipedes to hold off the pangs of starvation. Exhausted from the day in, day out search for food, no-one ever looked up. The normal three-hour midday

siesta reduced to almost nothing, they had to keep going to find enough food. It was then that they lost Gomina, the group's bundle of joy and Cicatrice's last remaining daughter, to the swift, frightening dive of a martial eagle. Spread out on the open, exposed river flats, each selfishly seeking his own food, Gomina as usual called madly to all those around for any extra food items they had. All that Cicatrice and Ugly now remember is the rapid rushing of air as the martial eagle dived terrorisingly down upon the group. There was

not time to even emit an alarm call. Gomina was gone, clenched between the long talons of the bird. At least her death was instantaneous.

Small, White, Petite Jaune and Parkinson his pal subsequently left the group. Their time had come to search out their own mates, another group and another home. This had left only Cicatrice, Ugly and two young bachelors that had come from an adjoining family. If they lost any more members, the group would not be able to patrol and defend the territory from their encroaching neigh-

For more than five years Alain Degré and Sylvie Robert lived with a group of meerkats in the Nossob region, in the very heart of the southern Kalahari. The book Meerkat Valley recounts their daily experiences with these delightful animals. Two years have elapsed since the publication of the book, and there have been many adventures . . .

bours, who, like them, were suffering from the lack of food and a constant harassment by chanting goshawks and jackals. But Cicatrice was carrying their insurance policy in her womb. If only she and her small, tired band could hold out for a few more months against the relentless, harsh Kalahari, just until the rains and the coming of juicy beetle larvae — they may be able to make it and survive.

That's now behind. Three litters, each with five strong babies, have been born in the meantime, seven of which stand around her and Ugly at the dens. For these young subadult meerkats life is still a joke, one constant game without responsibility.

But with her latest five-day-old new litter of babies, securely hidden away in the deep labyrinth of tunnels below them, the subadults' responsibility in baby-sitting and sentry duty must improve. They even forget how three of their brothers were taken one windy morning when the dust blocked their eyes and threw Ugly from his post atop the thorn log. The old jackal from over the dune had come too rapidly upon them: there was nothing they could do. At least the jackal is now dead and gone; he took his last chance at the lion kill in the riverbed.

The food is now more plentiful with the recent good rains and they need not dig deep into the sands for the larvae and barking geckos. The denser stands of new golden grass make sentry duty difficult. Trees and tall bushes always have to be scaled to keep a wary eye out for the mischievous two jackals that live down the valley. They make too many close sorties around the group, always on the trot as if going elsewhere, but in fact intent on them and the unsuspecting juveniles. They must watch and be careful.

The two tall strange human companions, Alain and Sylvie, are back among them. Allowed to walk with the group as they hunt, they scratch the juveniles and share the alarms and joys of their day. They pose no threat and even sometimes give the alarm, or provide shade under their tall figures on hot days. At least they keep the two jackals away. Chanting goshawks still come but more to see these two strangers.

Alain's and Sylvie's vehicle slowly moves towards the den. The heroes are still there, basking and enjoying the tranquil warmth of the early morning. When they come closer on foot the group glances and accepts them immediately. Some lie flat out on their stomachs, front paws outstretched, tenderly playing with sand in front of them. Others nibble and comb their long claws through each other's fur, uttering affectionate little cries of pleasure, expressing their bonds between each other.

A "bruuuurrrpp" emits from Cicatrice as she disappears down the hole, only to emerge with a small pink bundle between her teeth. She drops it at Alain's feet;

the baby lies motionless on the sand. Thinking it dead Alain picks the creature up, only to hear a squeak erupt from its "lifeless" body. It's alive but why give it to me? Immediately alert to the baby's cry a subadult runs over, clasps the baby between his teeth and drags it back down the hole, alarmed at his mother's behaviour and annoyed at the humans for delving into their privacy. Overwhelmed by the gesture to show and share the litter with the tall strange companion, Alain smiles at the closer, tender bond between man and meerkat.

Every day the babies grow stronger in the underground haven until one morning, while the group laps up and enjoys the early-morning warm-up, there suddenly appears a noisy miniature meerkat, wobbly on all fours and barely able to hold its tail erect. Stunned at the unexpected arrival Cicatrice drags it back down into the hole, only to find another four determined baby meerkats heading skyward. They have won their right to their first day above ground, in the hostile Kalahari's dust and sun, and the loving hugs and kisses of the group.

Striding out confidently, tail held high, the baby strikes out from the hole, only to be dragged back by the moaning and now exhausted babysitter.

Where are Cicatrice and Ugly and my lazy brothers, gone for what seems hours on their morning foraging trip? Rushing to the security of the crater mouth, baby swinging in his mouth, he stands and searches the sky and flat terrain around. No signs of the group, nor predators. Up pops another chirping baby determined to see more of this bright world above ground. Nosing the one and dragging the other escapee the baby-sitter steers the young down into the cool earth where they should remain. As he runs back up the burrow the blue sky draws closer and bigger. Above the burrow, alone at last, he stands. Suddenly the sand rushes at him as he hits the hole's edge. All goes dark.

At the new den, on the far edge of the valley, Alain and Sylvie wait patiently for signs of life. Slowly and nervously one head appears, glancing everywhere in rapid movements as the meerkat hesitantly moves to the hole's edge. Then appears another, and another, and finally Cicatrice. They all stand hunched over, heads hung low. Gone is their erect proud confidence and gone is one subadult.

Cicatrice's teats which stand dry and shrivelled on her belly tell more. The babies are missing as well — something has happened, the group is shattered. Approaching closer, the group glances nervously at Sylvie and Alain. Unsure and beaten they move closer together. Slowly and tenderly Sylvie strokes Cicatrice who moans quietly in her grief. Sylvie and Alain now understand why there was the sudden change in dens. It must have been the two jackals that killed the baby-sitter and the young as they came curiously one by one to investigate their new and exciting — but unknown to them, dangerous — world.

Away on the edge of the riverbed small clouds of dust attract a subadult's attention. His alarm bark and direction-

al gaze shock the group awake. Suddenly erect and different they all look towards the neighbouring group that has infiltrated their territory. Cicatrice's characteristic call rallies the group, who together bound off in the invaders' direction. Drawing closer, tails held stiffly forward like cannon barrels aiming at the enemy, the group begins the leap in unison, like a wave. Terrified by the sudden attack the invaders dash away up the dune and out of the heroes' valley. Exhilarated with their courageous behaviour and success, each meerkat marks the ground and small tussocks of short-legged Bushman grass where the invaders were foraging. Standing erect and proud Cicatrice gazes for an instant after the invaders. Another beep draws the group

together as they skip away on a much needed patrol around their beautiful valley. Self-confidence restored, they can now face the Kalahari again and look forward to the next bundles of joy — baby meerkats just three months away.

on very cold winter mornings. Living and dead plant matter can however absorb the increased amount of atmospheric moisture, so animals grazing upon these plants in the early morning can radically increase their water intake. This, together with the mild temperatures at night, explains why gemsbok and wildebeest both spend 60% of the night feeding, compared to a meagre 30% of the day. Of great importance is also the animals' ability to select good quality food items, such as greener leaves, from among the mass of poor quality, dry fibrous stems and leaves.

Inactivity by the vast majority of animals during the scorching hot part of the day is an important behavioural mechanism to survive in arid environments. Reduced exercise means a lower overall daily metabolism and a reduced loss of body water.

Behavioural observations I was making on gemsbok and wildebeest involved following them in a vehicle from sunrise to sunset. During hot summer days they went into the shade at about 10h00 and emerged only at about 16h00.

My San tracker and I regularly followed the tracks of groups and individual gemsbok and wildebeest to record what they ate and how it differed seasonally. Gemsbok with their smaller mouths and more flexible lips would in both summer and winter select more green vegetation than the wide-mouthed and unselective wildebeest. This, together with the gemsbok's ability to use the leaves of trees and bushes and dig for moisture-laden tubers, means that they can survive without surface drinking water, provided the food remains of relatively good quality.

Eland, hartebeest, springbok, steenbok and duiker are similar to gemsbok in their abilities to live without drinking water but they cannot compete with the other physiological adaptations of the gemsbok, which enable them to penetrate even to the shifting sands of the Namib desert. These species differences were further evidenced during a serious drought that occurred in 1985. The order in which the different antelope species succumbed to the exceedingly dry conditions reflected their different abilities to survive in this semi-arid region.

During the summer season of 1984/85 an average of 126 mm of rain fell in the Kalahari Gemsbok National park. The total of 20 showers recorded at Nossob camp included only five greater than 10 mm, and averaged 38 days apart! The vegetation that sprouted soon withered away in the increasingly hot, relentless sun. No tsamma melons germinated and all the signs looked disastrous for the Kalahari and its wildlife.

In June 1985 there was a sudden dramatic influx of wildebeest and eland into the southwestern section of the Kalahari Gemsbok National Park. They apparently came from the northeast of the Botswana Gemsbok National Park and surrounding areas, moving in small,

The cool shade of tussocks of grass provides a vantage point for the meerkat sentry during the daily foraging trip.

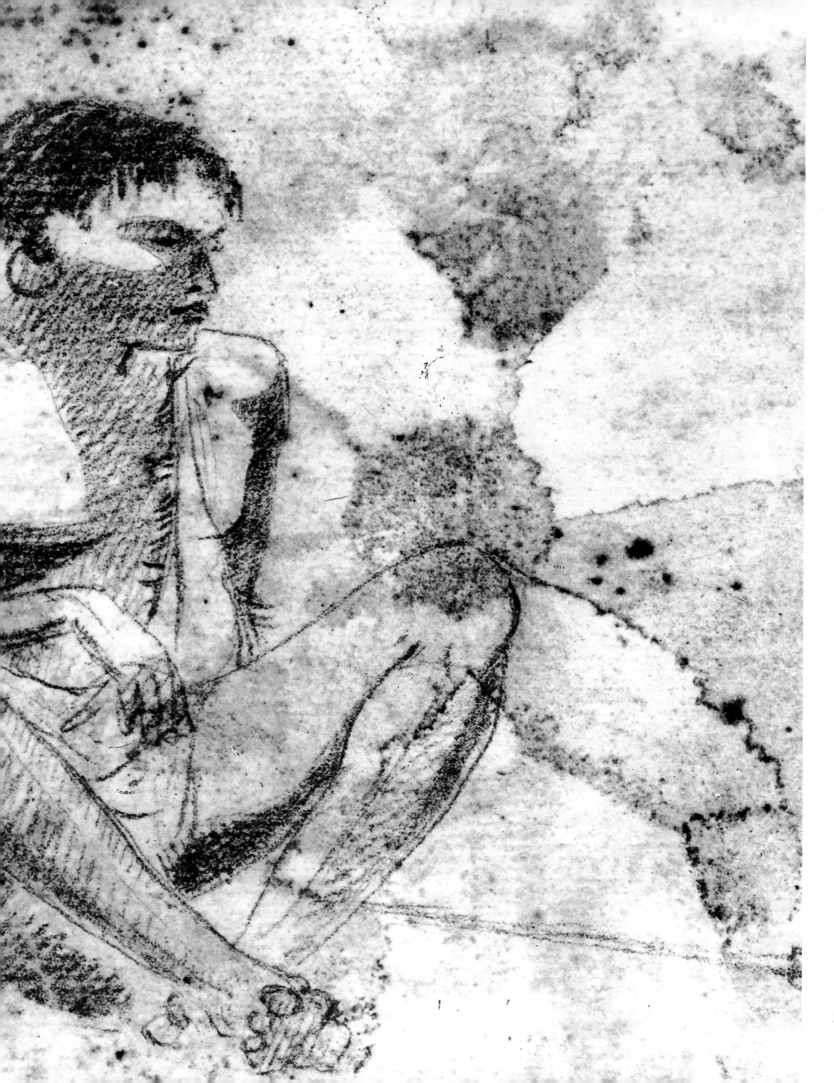

A brief ray of evening sun after the storm strangely illuminates the Nossob riverbed.

(Preceding pages) *Blanketed in beauty, the dunes are covered by dense stands of cat's tail or Herbstaedtia linearis after good rains.*

rather insignificant groups, which slowly drew closer together and became larger as they were funnelled together by the Park's southern boundary fence. At that time I had five eland and seven wildebeest equipped with radio-collars. They showed particularly restless behaviour, moving up and down along the southern fence of the Park and the Auob river.

Many mothers and calves became separated. Driving along the fence one frequently found young animals wandering in small groups or entirely on their own. The animals were weak, with protruding hips and ribs and sunken stomachs. Their coats were

Two petrified meerkats trying to locate the sound of thunder.
They will spend the rest of the day in their burrows.

Changing its skin colour from yellow to speckled green
when hunting and to grey when angered, the uncommon
common chameleon gently rocks like a leaf in its patient
search for insects in the dry southern Kalahari sands. It cannot, however, match the red colour of the sand as can its
brother, the dwarf Namaqua chameleon from the arid
wastes of Namaqualand.

dull and lifeless, the normal sheen of health gone. In some places frightened eland charged and flattened the southern game fence and continued their southward journey, showing no respect for the many, but much smaller, sheep fences that lay between them and the distant Orange river. Outside the main camp, Twee Rivieren, situated on the Nossob river, park rangers had to chase restless wildebeest herds back from the fence. Their attempt to push south appears to have been an ancient instinctive drive, or learned behaviour, passed down for generations to move in that direction, possibly to the Orange river 300 km in the distant south. The water may not have been the only driving force: they had moved past many artificial water points in their southward drive through the Park. The strong south wind against which they trekked may have also carried sweet scents of better grazing and other water points from the many farms in the south. But the farms were also denuded of vegetation, with sheep and cattle dying of hunger. Many farmers had to sell at very reduced prices up to 70% of their stock to save the herds, and themselves from financial ruin.

Farmers to the south of the Park hungrily began to capture the highly prized but weakened eland. Calves were easily caught and manhandled onto pick-up trucks and carted off to farms for fattening up and later selling, while adults were gently guided through deliberately collapsed game fences to capture the animals. In some places farmers even cut the southern border fence of Botswana and illegally crossed into the territory to round up and steal wandering eland. Wildebeest, on the other hand, considered a scourge by the farming community because they are known to spread certain domestic livestock diseases such as snotsiekte, were left to die in the parched sands or mercilessly shot because of their potential threat to the remaining grazing on the farms. Frequently one would see a lone, six month old wildebeest calf deserted and left to die. Sometimes they would desperately run after your passing vehicle and all you could do was go faster and lose them in the dust, but not from your mind. What could be done? We were witnessing the tragic death of the last remnants of the once great Kalahari herds of wildebeest and eland.

Driving in the dunes close to the Auob riverbed I remember seeing a group of six huge, grey-blue eland

Giant eagle owl chicks.

Each eye is independent of the other and can turn in all directions. When the chameleon spots an insect, both eyes turn to look in the same direction in order to judge the distance.

bulls, trotting as they do when disturbed, through the low, leafless brown bushes. Suddenly one of them collapsed. Thinking it had tripped in one of the many desert whistling rat burrows that infest the dunes, I stopped and waited to see the beautiful animal rise – but it did not. Approaching slowly on foot I saw the bull lying on his side, legs outstretched and his one thick horn stuck back into the sand supporting his heavy head above the sand surface. There was no whistling rat hole or any other holes in the area – he had just collapsed from weakness and exhaustion. The animal eyed me with his unblinking, slightly bulging eyes as I drew closer, but he did not flinch a muscle as I carefully clasped his horns. To lift the huge 700 kg eland alone I knew was impossible but heave as much as I physically could I was not even able to raise his head. What frustrated me most was that the eland did not even try to get up. It had given up the struggle, the will to live was no longer there. That was June, another five months of progressively worse conditions and suffering lay ahead before the first, hopeful rains would fall, but this eland bull did not even see the moon rise that night. The jackals had plucked his eyes out and torn his testicles off before his great heart stopped pumping.

The next day, I saw an eland cow and wildebeest bull suffer the same fate. The scene was set for a disastrous drought and die-off in the southern Kalahari.

Driving through the carnage I recorded the progression of the die-off. Stopping at every carcass Hermanus and I saw, we would note the species, sex and age, and if only a few days old, the quality of the bone marrow, which indicated the animal's body condition at the time of death. Around some of the boreholes, and notably the more salty ones, up to 50 wildebeest carcasses at a time were recorded. Animals suffering from chronic thirst and starvation are unable to cope with salt water as it further dehydrates them, which in turn increases their craving for the water, so the vicious circle rapidly accelerates towards death.

In the early stages of the drought, the majority of carcasses were those of wildebeest. More specifically they consisted of old wildebeest bulls and young calves. Cows no longer able to suckle deserted their dependent calves while the old bulls, pushed out to the poorer grazing, could not manage the poor quality, tough grasses with their inefficient, worn-out teeth. Moving into the shade, they quietly awaited their fate.

By October, the rapidly worsening heat and ever drier veld took its toll on eland, hartebeest and ostrich, in that order. Like the wildebeest, first the old animals and young calves died, but later all ages began to succumb. And in the final stages of the drought old gemsbok and springbok also began to die. Many of these dying animals, lying in the shade or standing around the boreholes with heads hung low, could be approached and touched. They were too weak to be startled: to move was too much of an effort.

Cheetah cubs.

oor (short ear), two old male lions with a long history in the Nossob camp area, were saved from a certain death by the drought. Just prior to the die-off these two males were in terrible condition with sunken, wrinkled stomachs, short tatty manes, and front and hindquarters withered away. They were also without a pride as they had been evicted by two young males a few months earlier. I saw them the day they stole a drought-stricken wildebeest bull from a single lioness, after not eating anything for well over a week. I was able to approach within 2 m of the carcass but they would not budge and did not even offer a snarl or mock charge as usual. The closer I drew the faster they tore at the wildebeest flesh. They survived a further two years in the area and even regained their pride for a short while before disappearing for ever into the sands.

Vulture numbers increased in the area and they became plentiful down the Auob river where they had not often been recorded. But as so many animals were dying simultaneously, not half the carcasses were opened by the larger carnivores. Within 48 hours the dry atmosphere dried and hardened the skin, preserving the victim's last struggling posture for months to come. Thus jackals and vultures were denied access into the carcasses. Often even our sharpened axe could not break the iron-hard skin, it just bounced back however hard you wielded it.

We can only guess at the actual number of animals that died. Around the waterholes and along the roads within the Park nearly 2 000 carcasses were examined and another 1 700 were counted from the air, but many died deep in the shade of trees and in the surrounding farming areas away from our searching eyes. The die-off was however very small in comparison to other such events that occurred elsewhere in the Kalahari over the last 50 years. A huge die-off occurred in 1930, and again in 1961 and 1964, when as many as 80 000 wildebeest alone died along newly erected foot-and-mouth cordon fences in the central Kalahari. In 1979 and 1983 more than 40 000 wildebeest died, plus an untold number of hartebeest, giraffe and gemsbok. It is true that these had been years of poor rains, but the other major factor common to all these disasters was the presence of man. The concentration of people around the important permanent water sources denies the wildlife undisturbed access to the water; unrealistically large domestic stock numbers compete for the limited grazing around the water; the erection of farm and veterinary fences cuts animals' natural migration routes. All this contributed greatly to the die-offs, which otherwise could have been largely avoided.

In the southern Kalahari, nothing can be done to provide access for these animals to the Orange river. The distance of 300 km is too great and involves too much farmland; besides, relinquishing the land for wildlife would not be justifiable when it may only periodically be used. Therefore, if it was only water these migrating animals were after, provision has

Lions, leopards, hyaenas and jackals capitalised on the situation, catching these bags of bones without any effort. One of my collared lions, an old male, killed four eland and two wildebeest in one night at the same waterhole. He ate only the heart, lungs and liver – the best parts of each carcass – as the remaining muscle was virtually useless. Victor and Stomp-

(Left) It only takes $\frac{1}{16}$th of a second for the chameleon's tongue to reach its prey. It can extend its tongue further than its body is long – the only creature with such a tongue.

been made in the form of boreholes scattered throughout the South African Kalahari Gemsbok National Park. But food, also in short supply in times of drought, can only be guaranteed through thoughtful management of the water supplies. This means moving the wildebeest population, the species most dependent on drinking water, around the Park by closing certain waterholes and opening others.

Droughts, even though terrible and costly in animal life, are a phenomenon the land can endure: they are part of a process by which animal and plant populations are greatly reduced after a build-up in numbers. We should, however, be aware of man's great influence in the sequence of events. So we must learn from the previous die-offs and plan accordingly for the next drought – it may be our last chance to save the once great herds of the Kalahari from extinction.

Where these migratory wildebeest and eland came from has been the subject of much speculation. Similar concentrations had occurred in the southern Kalahari before, but irregularly. In August 1979 a huge gathering of an estimated 90 000 wildebeest and 2 500 eland was found in the central regions of the South African Park. They moved out a short while later in a southeasterly direction, later turning to the northeast, and were spotted by Mark Owens while he was flying in the Central Kalahari Game Reserve in Botswana. This herd met its fate on the Kuke veterinary cordon fence that prevented it from getting to the waters of the Boteti river and lake Xau. Another but much smaller concentration of the remnant wildebeest population occurred in the Molopo region of southern Botswana in June 1980. Again in September 1981, May 1983 and June 1985 wildebeest, eland and hartebeest concentrated in the South African Park.

Radio-tracking of collared wildebeest individuals has revealed that there appears to be two populations of wildebeest in the southern Kalahari. One remains resident within the South African Gemsbok Park, using the available borehole water points and keeping predominantly along the two fossil riverbeds. The other much larger population is entirely nomadic, moving over a larger area and surviving on green vegetation and tsamma melons elsewhere in the southern Kalahari and southern reaches of the central Kalahari. Occurring in small groups scattered over the whole region their numbers appear insignificant until they mass into groups of over 90 000.

Eland movements are similar: they also move in a huge circle within the southern Kalahari. As the winter veld begins to dry and the browse loses its leaves in the Gemsbok National Park, Mabuasehube Game Reserve and surrounding woodland areas, the eland move slowly in a southwesterly direction towards the large perennial grasslands and evergreen trees in the drier southwest section of the southern Kalahari, where they normally remain until the first rains in November, after which they return to Botswana for the sprouting grass, annuals and new browse.

The sinking red sun, made ever more fiery by the dusty air, awakens the creatures of the night. The silence of the now still and breathlessly hot twilight air is suddenly broken by a "click-click" close by, then another, then more further away, until the surrounding sands come alive with the chorus. As you move to locate the cause of the sound, the area immediately around you falls silent. Waiting patiently soon brings another "click-click" close by: it is from the small, burrowing barking gecko *Ptenopus garrulus*. From just inside their burrow entrances these aggressive, vocal little geckos bark to advertise their presence to surrounding competitors and receptive females. Restricted entirely to the Kalahari sands, these geckos have barks that vary between species, individuals and even with the humidity, temperature and the amount of light at night. They bark only in summer during

The Kori bustard, the largest flying bird, with a mass of up to 19 kg, uses riverbeds, pans and red sand dune habitats extensively. They forage over great distances for insects, lizards and rodents.

twilight at sunset and sunrise and throughout the night on full moon. Hunting from their burrow, they wait for insects to come to them, which they dash out to collect and drag back to their haven in the sand where they remain safe from jackals, Cape foxes, owls and other larger sand geckos that prey upon them.

With the more amiable night temperatures the Kalahari sands become a hive of activity. Sand temperature on the surface declines from the 70° C experienced in mid-afternoon to around 23° C in the evening. The nocturnal rodents such as the hairy-footed gerbil *Gerbillurus paeba* scurry among the bushes searching for seeds, much like their diurnal compatriots. Between bushes they move more rapidly for fear of those silently flying nocturnal raptors, the owls. Special barbs on the owls' soft feathers muffle the flap of their wings, making their flight almost soundless. The bipedal or hopping means of locomotion allows the gerbils to move quickly into the open sandy areas to sift rapidly for seeds before fleeing to the dark bushes for safety. The slower-moving quadrupedal rodents like the short-tailed gerbil *Desmodillus auricularis* and the large-eared mouse *Malacothrix typica* move slowly in their search for food. The former species has enlarged bullae in the ear and can detect the silent flap of flying owls. Both species freeze when alarmed and thus often escape detection as they forage on the more exposed pan and riverbed surfaces.

THE REBIRTH

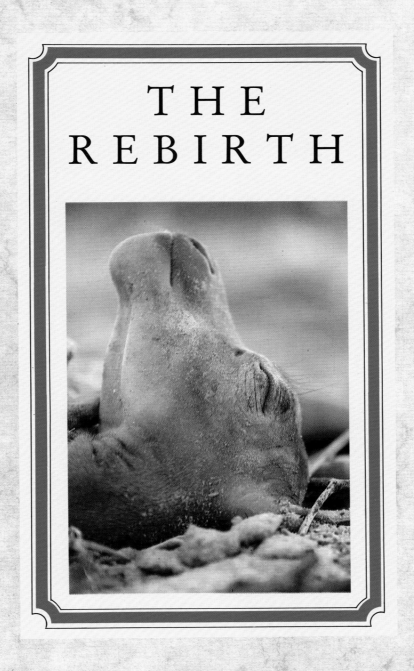

The male black korhaan raucously expounds his presence to neighbours, potential rivals and females alike.

For an hour now, I have been sitting in the moonlight with my head resting on the steering wheel, waiting. The few nearby golden tussocks of Bushman grass gently blink in the soft, blue light that blankets the flat, naked sides to the Nossob riverbed. No sound pollutes the Kalahari night, except for the gentle squeak of my open driver's door and the soft breathing of Hermanus, who lies outstretched in the back of the open truck. Above, the stars bright and majestic paint the heavens and act as my guides. The Southern Cross, Orion's Belt, Seven Sisters, Scorpio and the Milky Way dividing the high November sky lead us through the featureless dune sea at night.

The sudden, loud "kree-kree-krieep-kreeip" of an alarmed crowned plover seems to jerk the truck as Hermanus startles awake. Out of the grass near us, only Olivia's head is briefly raised to scan the open riverbed, before she resettles it back on her outstretched paws. The other four spotted hyaenas: Goldie, Lorna, Hans and Moony, remain motionless and unperturbed by the disturbance.

Since sunset this evening I have followed these five members of the Kousaunt spotted hyaena clan on one of their foraging trips. Not worried by my closely trailing, noisy vehicle they go about their normal nightly duties. But so far tonight, as last night, they have done nothing more than move a kilometre or so, lie down for a while and again move on a short way before lying down once more.

Olivia's alarm drum, a soft low-pitched growling sound, brings all members of the group to their feet in

The majestic bateleur, exterminated from most of southern Africa, finds refuge in the remote reaches of the southern Kalahari.
(Overleaf) Scattered thunderstorms drop their precious loads on the southern Kalahari plains, giving them life in patches. Animals and people alike move towards these storms in the hope of finding drinking water.

an instant. The two slowly advancing cheetah stop in their tracks about 15 m away, apparently unaware of the hyaenas near the vehicle. Tails raised and cocked forward, all five hyaenas immediately give chase to the cheetahs, who quickly dash away, then stop and look back, while the slower hyaenas continue their pursuit. Seeing the hyaenas' determination, the cheetahs again dash away into the grassy flats, well away from the aggressive hyaenas. When I finally catch up to them, 500 m away, they are all noisily greeting and licking each other, probably a triumphant handshake and pat on the back for their successful chase of one of their potential competitors. Hans's "whooop", repeated seven times, cuts and bounces through the silent night. Jackals in the distance reply but there is not a sound from other members of the clan.

As if suddenly awakened by this excitement, they spread out and begin moving slowly northwards along the riverbank. Following slowly 10 m behind with only the orange parking lights on and the Southern Cross over my right shoulder, Hermanus and I bounce along, keeping a beady eye on the one individual immediately ahead. Every now and then all members begin to lope gracefully, thus covering a greater distance in shorter time. Frequently they hold their heads high and sniff the air for smells of carcasses or prey species.

Veering to the left, they suddenly run, fast, into the riverbed. Following closely behind in their dust and flying sand, I flash the headlights intermittently to watch the running hyaenas and avoid the now rapidly approaching trees and stumps. The amount of dust increases. Now and then the black hoof of a fleeing wildebeest flashes in the light, as the closely packed wildebeest herd run at 40 km/h onto the flat grassy riverbank, with the hyaenas trying to separate a

ARRIVAL AT THE WATER PIT (Sept. 6, 1861).

UNDERGROUND HOMES AND THEIR INHABITANTS

As in all arid regions, water and food are limited. The rodents show fascinating adaptations to live in the wastelands and maximise these limited resources.

Most of the 17 recorded rodent species in the southern Kalahari are active only at night, thus escaping the hottest and most demanding period of the day in the safety of a burrow in the sands. Besides providing physical protection from predators, the burrow also acts as a buffer against the harsh environment. The radical temperature fluctuations experienced above ground are not felt in burrows deeper than 30 cm. The almost totally sealed, cool environment also has much higher relative humidity than there is above ground. This is of immense importance to burrowing animals as it means that they do not inhale dry air, and thus do not lose excessive amounts of body water through evaporation as occurs in the desiccating conditions above ground. Hence the utilisation of burrows is of great biological significance in regulating an animal's water balance. Animals from the minute 5 g pygmy mouse to the large 50 kg antbear construct and use burrows and could not survive in the arid Kalahari environment without them. Sometimes antbear holes, through frequent use over the years by antbears themselves and by porcupines, form huge, wide-mouthed pits in which a vehicle would comfortably disappear. Steenbok, leopards, spotted and brown hyaenas and even humans frequently use these cool retreats to escape the merciless summer sun and freezing winter nights.

Besides mammals, several birds species such as the ant-eating chat *Myrmecocichla formicivora* and swallow-tailed bee-eater *Merops hirundineus* use burrows in the sands to roost and breed in, as do a myriad of insects.

The overall reduction of body metabolism is also an important adaptation to surviving in arid environments, and is particularly common among the rodents. It means a reduced food demand — important, as food is generally scarce — plus a reduced overall loss of body water, less activity above ground and hence less exposure to predation. Some rodents, such as the pouched mouse, allow their body temperature to drop by 10° C to 15° C, a phenomenon known as torpor. When inactive in this way they save even more energy and water. Often on winter mornings when live-trapping rodents I would find pouched mice in this state in the traps. Holding them in your hand they sluggishly move their legs and body as they slowly warm up and begin to arouse.

Torpor is known to occur in Africa's smallest predatory bird, the 60 g pygmy falcon *Polihierax semitorquatus*, which nests in one of the many compartments in the huge sociable weaver nests, the biggest in the world. These massive communal nests which hang from cross-branches of large trees provide a relatively stable temperature into which the birds escape when conditions become either hot or cold. On cold winter nights up to three pygmy falcons huddle in a single compartment keeping each other warm, conserving body heat and energy. By dropping their body temperature slightly they conserve even more.

yearling from the herd. Goldie rushes past the herd to make it turn, in the hope that one will split away, but the herd stays tightly packed. After an 800 m chase the hyaenas stop and let the wildebeest canter off into the moonlight; a white trail marks their escape.

Turning towards the west, Olivia and Goldie lead the others towards the dunes. A series of distant whoops further to the west set them all in a lope. Sniffing the air, they move slightly to the south and begin to move faster. Much louder, faster whoops and giggles are now distinctly heard. Dashing down the dune slope the five startle other hyaenas feeding on a gemsbok calf. Recognition leads to groans and giggles of greeting as they tear at the freshly killed carcass. Once they calm down, I focus on each animal with my binoculars to determine who the other five individuals are. It is Koo...Guy, Ella, Nie and Heather – all adults of the clan are now together and accounted for.

Before first light the carcass is completely devoured. Olivia, Goldie and Nie, now bloated from their feast, begin their 10 km trek to their den where their small cubs await them. The others remain, content to laze out the coming hot day under the good

Kalahari to the elements. Rodents such as the striped mouse actively search for seed pods and blossoms under and within the many bushes, thus benefitting from the shade and the protection against the ever watchful pale chanting goshawks, bateleurs and martial eagles that glide quietly above. Other rodents such as the ground squirrels prefer to forage in open areas, in the riverbeds and at the edges of pans. They actually carry their shade around with them in the form of a bushy tail that they hang over themselves while feeding. With their slightly protruding eyes they keep a constant look-out for jackals, Cape foxes and predatory birds. Once it gets too hot in the open the squirrels rush into the closest shade, lie on their bellies with legs stretched forward and backward, and throw cool sand over themselves, thus transferring the heat to the cooler ground and sand. Suricates and yellow mongooses practise the same behaviour to cool themselves while foraging on hot days. Hyaenas lie in shallow excavations under trees and often urinate on the sand to help the cooling effect.

Others, such as the whistling rat, never venture further than a few metres from one of their many burrow entrances. On seeing a piece of green grass or leaf

Bateleur.

A ground squirrel carcass.

shade bushes scattered on the surrounding dunes.

Towards the brightening sky the three females, and we, wearily move. Barking geckos all along our route wish the fading darkness well with their loud chorus of barks. The slowly rising, fiery red sun, symbol of the new day, sets alight the Kalahari's hope yet again. Small puffs of orange cloud dot the distant northern horizon. Every day for the last week the strongly blowing northerly wind has brought these clouds of vapour and hope of rain, but by mid-afternoon each day they have fizzled away, leaving only the blazing sun and scorching November heat.

Sunrise sees a hive of activity involving small and large, as within a few hours the intense heat will push them into their shaded, cooler havens, leaving the

close to the ground it scurries out, chops it off and drags the morsel back to its burrow entrance where it consumes it in the safe, cool micro-climate. Once it becomes very hot the whistling rats oscillate between the entrances and the labyrinth of tunnels below the bushes. Because of the many entrances there is a cool through-flow of air in the tunnels. In many places these tunnel systems are so extensive and the whistling rats' impact on the bushes above so great that whole stands of black thorn are undermined. Besides partially controlling bush encroachment, the construction of these large burrow systems helps aerate the soil, while the rats' faeces, stored bedding and items of food fertilise the soil. Sitting in or next to the burrow entrances, they remain constantly alert and

Ground squirrels, fight over a small piece of water-rich tsamma melon.

once a predator is seen they whistle, informing the hungry enemy that its dangerous game has been exposed.

By mid-morning the ever increasing heat brings the towering columns of red dust, the wind devils, that crazily lean forward and make their way over the shimmering red sands. Roaring as they pass closely by, they whip the sand, dust and hot air up into the heavens – and are gone as quickly as they came. Heat waves distort the air and create shimmering mirages of floating trees and springbok grazing around pans. Undeterred by the heat, cicadas with their ear-piercing shrieks, characteristic of the hot African bush, merrily sing from every large *Acacia* tree.

Those animals unable to escape from the intense heat into burrows below the ground find shade under the trees. Springbok, wildebeest, lions and sheep all cluster, separately, under trees and follow the shade around, while single gemsbok and hartebeest lie under smaller bushes. Birds settle deep within the canopies and some, such as the turtle and Namaqua doves, even roost on the ground in the shade next to the stem. Within each tree there are convective currents, hot air rising on the hotter periphery of the canopy while within the shaded central areas cooler air currents flow down to the ground.

However, the use of trees and large holes for shade can often prove a painful experience: living in the loose sands under well-used trees are blood-sucking tick-like creatures known as sand tampans. More frequently active during the warm summer months, this tick lurks in the cool sands under trees and actively seeks out any mammal looking for relief from the heat in the shade. Tampans detect their potential host through carbon dioxide detectors on the first set of appendages, known as pedipalps. Holding these up above their bodies they test the air and rapidly home in on the unsuspecting victim, sometimes in their hundreds. Their saliva contains a mild neurotoxin that anaesthetises the bite area, making it almost undetectable. Young, aged or sick animals can become

Sick and old animals are often selected by predators, but the jackal kills many springbok lambs as well.

(Right) *Able hunters and scavengers, black-backed jackals adapt to all situations. Hated by sheep farmers because they sometimes kill lambs, they are hunted down with dogs or at night with spotlights.*

When a lioness is in oestrus mating can take place every half hour, day and night, for several days.

PHOTO BY MICHAEL KNIGHT

(Above) The ancient dry Nossob riverbed cuts through the naked dunes, the legacy of too many goats and sheep outside the southern limit of the Kalahari Gemsbok National Park. **(Opposite)** Electrified game fences extend down the western and southern borders of the Kalahari Gemsbok National Park. Fences were initially erected to prevent game moving into adjacent farms; electrified strands were later added to deter lions, leopards and caracal from leaving the Park and harassing the adjacent sheep and cattle. But holes dug by antbear and porcupine frequently undermine the fences and let jackals and lions through. In retaliation farmers often set "gin traps" to trap the transgressors, such as this unfortunate porcupine.

paralysed when bitten by enough tampans. One Kalahari farmer reported removing 13 ℓ of engorged tampans from three cows which died from loss of blood. The blood-sucking process must be quickly completed while the host remains in the shade: dropping off onto the hot sand would be fatal for the tampans, as they cannot tolerate exposure to direct sunlight or sand temperatures above 55°C. This explains why large trees with, in our opinion, suitable shade are often avoided in favour of smaller, less efficient shade-giving bushes and trees.

During my first visit to the Kalahari sands, I could not understand why, during siesta, Gus Mills and Hermanus wanted to rest on their truck. Ten minutes of sitting on the ground was enough to tell me why.

Interestingly, Hodson, a tax collector and renowned hunter in the Bechuanaland Protectorate at the turn of the century, noted an almost complete lack of tampans in the central and southern Kalahari sands, a far cry from today's situation. Their scarcity then may have resulted from overall lower game and livestock numbers and the highly nomadic nature of the large antelope. Today's provision of drinking water and higher, more resident game populations within the national parks, and with more livestock outside, may have encouraged a simultaneous boom in the

antelope and carnivores have difficulty keeping their body temperatures down to the normal 37° C. Lions and hyaenas salivate, lick their legs and fur and pant heavily to keep cool, losing precious body water. The large antelope, such as the eland and gemsbok, can stop sweating altogether and allow their body temperature to rise above 42° C for up to eight hours, thus saving an immense amount of body water. In such circumstances the heat in fact flows from the animal to the environment – a favourable situation. However, such high body temperatures are normally lethal to most mammals, as the delicate brain is not suited to such extremes. Therefore, the eland and gemsbok and most other arid-adapted antelope have a highly sophisticated cooling device situated below the brain to keep the sensitive tissues cool and active, while letting the remainder of the body heat up.

With the now stronger northerly winds, again comes the choking dust. The intense heat and now soaring humidity make conditions almost unbearable. White clouds, increased in number and size, bring welcome shade as they drift slowly across the sky. A few begin to bulge and billow as they grow rapidly upwards, becoming darker by the minute. A deep, menacing blue colour develops in the western sky. The winds pick up with sudden violence, blow-

tampan population and distribution. In fact today they pose a serious economic threat to the livestock industry in the Kalahari sands.

With shade temperatures soaring to 38° and 40° C, still several degrees lower than in the sun, the large

The remarkable and peculiar anatomical character of the San: steatopygia. Fat accumulates in the buttocks to form a vital reserve for use in an environment where poor nutrition is the norm.

ing from left to right and back again. Lightning is seen but not heard, then again and again as the black mass aggressively lashes out at the tired famished land. The fiery red, naked dune crests stand out in defiance against the marching storm. The horizon disappears entirely behind black streaks of hard rain in the distance. Thunder now booms out across the limp landscape and the black clouds roll onward. The winds, now even more violent, buckle and flatten the parched grass on the sand, rent and shake the tough camel-thorns, tearing branches from their supports.

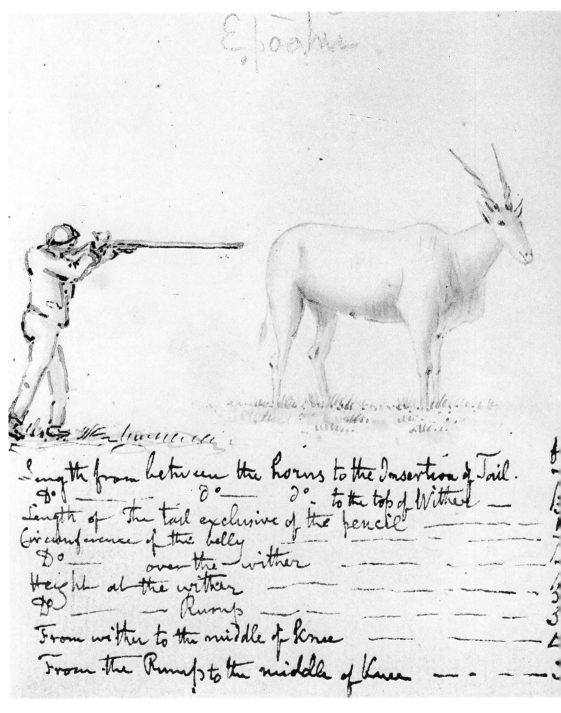

(Below) An old battle-scarred gemsbok bull picks and chooses his way through the dry grasslands as he patrols his large territory. By a combination of reduced activity during the heat of the day, feeding mainly at night and selecting the better quality grass and tree leaves gemsbok can survive without drinking water.

"In the afternoon, I observed with my telescope one of the hunters on horseback, following an eland which was coming towards us. It is the practice to drive their game as near home as possible before it is shot but this cannot easily be done till, by a long chase, the animal begins to flag. This was the case at present, and the Hottentot drove it on before him with as much ease as he might have driven a cow. The

21

357

p.14.9.11.

	ft. in
From the hind knee to point of hoof — — —	2 . 3 .
From the fore knee to the point of the hoof — — —	1 . 6½
Diameter of fore knee in profile — — —	. A
Diam of hind knee .do — — —	. 7½
a "little below (thinnest part) — — —	. 3½
a little below the fore knee — — —	. 2¾
Profile Diam of Fore thigh next the body — —	. 8
do — — — hinder thigh .do — — —	. 9½

(Overleaf) Gemsbok flock to the green riverbeds for their nutritious grasses and salt licks but also to escape the irritating secretions of the dense stands of sour grass Schmidtia kalahariensis that cover the dune country. After a long stay in the dunes, animals no longer show the beautiful, contrasting black and white leg and facial patterns but a dirty dull-grey colour from the grass secretions. These secretions can cause eye irritations, swollen tongues and lesions on the legs.

animal was brought within twenty yards of the wagons, where it stood still, unable from fatigue to move a step further. Before the hunter fired again, he was persuaded to wait till I had made two sketches . . ." as described by W. Burchell.

(Right) Once the antelope has been divided among the members of the clan, the hunters prepare the biltong.

SIP-WELLS
AND PUTS

The San make use of "sip-wells", but they are scarce. They do not provide much water, yet enough to save a life. Locating a damp place by characteristic plant growth the San women, who are responsible for collecting water and plants, excavate a shallow hole. Into this they pack a small clump of grass or roots into which a hollow grass stalk is stuck. The hole is filled in and firmly tramped down around the protruding grass stalk. Returning a while later the women will suck on the reed for sometimes over an hour, creating a negative pressure in the grass clump and drawing a slow dribble of water up the stalk. Water collected like this, if not immediately drunk, is stored in empty ostrich shells that are buried for later use. During the early lawless times of the southern Kalahari, thirsty and desperate hunters and even police are known to have held San people at gunpoint to discover their hidden stores of ostrich eggs.

Sometimes fairly shallow conventional wells or "puts" are sunk into the sands to tap water trapped on a shallow calcrete shelf, but they are rare and occur only in good rainfall years. I remember one instance when, flying low-level deep into the Botswana section of the Park after a radio-collared vulture, I suddenly saw a few goats, then several donkeys run from be-neath shade on the southern edge of a huge pan in an area where no people were meant to be or known to live. How could these water-dependent animals survive here without drinking water – the pan had been dry for six months and there were no tsammas in the area? Circling back and closely scrutinising the flat country adjacent to the pan's large southern sand dune, I noticed well-worn animal tracks leading to a small naked mound of sand a short way off. Descending even lower and swooping over the mound brought two men and a dog scurrying to the surface of the shallow excavation, not more than 4 m deep, from which they had been drawing water in small buckets. Landing on the pan to enquire what exactly they were doing in this area would not have helped, as they would simply have disappeared into the dunes. So I resorted to another low, fast swoop to chase them away from the Park, where they had no right to be with their livestock.

The first white and Baster farmers in the southern Kala-hari generally sank much deeper conventional wells in the calcrete on the edge of pans and riverbeds where water was normally found trapped. Some families, such as the Rautenbachs from Rietfontein, specialised in well digging, sometimes go-ing down 50 m, suspended by "riempies" or tough gemsbok hide strips while digging the well by hand. But some old wells, such as occur along the upper Nossob riverbed, were nothing more than shallow excavations to hold rainwater for short periods while the farmers grazed their sheep and cattle in the area before returning to permanent water sources. But as drinking

A once splendid Kalahari lion has gone through the cycle of life from beautiful and majestic in his prime, through old age, alone, to the final wait for death.

water is of utmost importance in this thirst-land, where horses frequently died under their riders on hot summer days, wells or "puts" took on a special meaning and became congregation points for hunters, farmers, explorers and future settlements.

The old maps displayed vast empty, uncharted expanses of sand cut through by the lifelines of dry riverbeds: the Molopo, Nossob, Auob and Kuruman, and scattered pans on which were dotted the "puts" and their names. Close on the map but sometimes days apart on horseback or in a bumpy donkey-cart were places with tongue-twisting names such as Zwartmodder, Abiquasputs, Middelputs, Geelputs, Noenieputs, Obogorop and Rietfontein, with their often brackish waters which tasted much sweeter after a few days in the Kalahari sun.

One of the most frequently used old Kalahari routes was the one from Upington via Zwartmodder and Abiquasputs to Rietfontein, over the border into German South-West Africa and on to Aroab and Keetmanshoop. To cover the 170 miles or 274 km from Upington to Rietfontein took seven days in a donkey cart or 36 hours on camel. But even with the signs of a road and scattered puts men frequently died of thirst.

A young Irish trooper named McShane of the Cape Mounted Police, returning from Zwartmodder to his isolated post at Nakob — he had reported the death of a San woman of thirst — lost his own horse after dismounting for a break. He followed the horse's tracks as his only water supply was attached to the saddle, but it was not long before the December heat drove him into the shade. In the meantime his horse had been located near Zwartmodder, and San trackers were hastily sent back on the horse's tracks to find the desperate policeman. Speed was of the essence as they all knew that if he was not soon located in the summer heat it would be too late.

From the policeman's tracks the San trackers could later describe McShane's desperate journey on foot. As he became weaker his tracks began to wander, circle back and cross his own path. He frequently collapsed in the shade of bushes or trees. Partially recovered he would briskly step out but soon begin to wander again until he had no clue where he was. He was found on the side of a dune where he had apparently died peacefully. The Kalahari sun had taken its toll in only three days.

The roar approaches closer and closer and now there is the first smell of manna from heaven, rain. The first in seven hard dry months. Springbok and wildebeest cluster closer together as they stand in awe of the approaching spectacle, beautiful in its harshness. The first huge, supercooled drops knock up minute clouds of dust as they slam into the soft, naked riverbed. Then quickly they increase to a torrent, stinging where they hit one's body. Everything goes grey and dull in the heavy rain. Springbok with heads hung low, tails between their legs and backs to the downpour look dejected and miserable. Martial eagles and many small birds alike seek refuge under

slowly begin to fill with the water rushing in from the edges. Every drop falling on the red sand is immediately swallowed by the thirsty sand, turning an even deeper red in colour. Animal tracks that once littered the sands are beaten and distorted into submission until they disappear completely into the wet sands.

The sky brightens and hot sunshine streaks in through the rain, now less heavy. As quickly as it came, the black cloud moves on to the southeast. Two fully arched rainbows mark its onward course and direction; the huge cloud, booming with thunder, rolls on to dump the rest of its precious load elsewhere.

About 150 lions live inside the National Park.

and next to branches deep in the tree canopies, anything to escape the hard, but wonderful, drops of life-giving water.

Small rivulets begin to flow from the white river-banks into the grey dead riverbed. What were once dust bowls rapidly begin to fill up with black, sludgy mud. The pans at first drink up the moisture but then

All around the Kalahari stands paralysed and dazed by the event. Trees, bushes and the sands, released of their layers of dust, sparkle clean and washed. Erecting their white pronks the springbok shake the water from their bodies, then take their first sips of summer rain. Lions and jackals emerge from their soaked refuges to see a clean, new Kalahari.

Pools of water lie in the riverbed and pans. Springbok and wildebeest, unaccustomed to the feel of water around their hooves, lift their legs high as they precariously slip and slide their way through the shallow pools. Forktailed drongos soon begin their noisy welcome to the rain: the new beginning, the time of new life in the Kalahari.

Elsewhere animals have seen, smelt and heard the rain but not felt it. The localised storm missed them in its uncharted course over the sands. Their Kalahari sand still remains dry and thirsty, but their time will also come. Springbok, wildebeest, eland and even people from afar begin moving towards the patch of

hope, in search of sweeter, better grasses, leaves and water. Turtle doves, laughing doves and sandgrouse, attracted from afar by the dark clouds, lightning and smell, head towards the veils of distant rain. Those too small to undertake such an arduous journey remain and continue as normal: their time will come. The trees, bushes and grasses likewise can only wait.

With these first rains the large eland herds immediately start moving out of the drier southwestern reaches of the Kalahari to the northeast. Tracking the movements of these antelope by monitoring a few radio-collared animals shows that they can cover well over 250 km in a week. Over the desolate sands the use of an aircraft is imperative in conducting such a study. Monitoring also the movement patterns of other collared animals: gemsbok, hartebeest, wildebeest, springbok, lions, leopards, cheetah and spotted hyaenas, as I have been doing for the last four years, has helped develop a more complete picture of how the large mammal community functions through the seasons of the southern Kalahari. With the aid of an aircraft I can plot the positions of up to 40 individual animals fitted with radio-collars in 12 hours of flying – that is, if they have all behaved and not moved off great distances!

The coming of the rains often proves a trying time for tracking. The eland, a few gemsbok and some wildebeest start moving well away from their haunts of the previous few months. In such circumstances I would fly wider and wider circles deeper into Botswana in the hope of locating these "lost" individuals.

This is also the time of year when the unstable weather conditions play havoc on my stomach and senses. A Kalahari thunderstorm from the ground is majestic and beautiful but from the air it can be a terrifying experience. Often after leaving base camp in Nossob in the morning on a flight deep into the Botswana sands, I would have to sneak and swivel my way back dodging the gusting winds and torrential rains that accompany these thunderstorms. The strong up-and-down thrusting winds can shear the wings off a light aircraft as easily as tearing a paper bag. Freezing conditions in the cloud itself can pack ice onto the wings, propellers and windscreen in a few minutes, making the aircraft virtually unflyable. So the rule that has saved me to date is to steer clear of the storms – or rather, at least to try. If one has to make a precautionary landing, the Kalahari offers enough room and opportunity, but the chances of walking away unscathed from an undamaged aircraft are slim. The pans and fossil riverbeds offer ideal landing strips but they are few and far between and are often rutted with lick sites. Once muddy or inundated they become an immediate death-trap for an aircraft. But it is not so much the landing that worries me. The chances are very slim that you will be spotted on the ground, even with signal flares, as the area is so vast and featureless that navigation is a bit of a thumb-suck. So a radio-collar and rifle goes with me everywhere: in case of an emergency I just activate the collar and wait for the searching aircraft to find my position.

On one occasion I attempted to rush from Twee Rivieren to Nossob ahead of an approaching storm. Fifteen minutes out from Twee Rivieren I realised I

(Preceding pages) *The Orange river lily Crinum bulbispermum. Rain transforms the dry Kalahari grasslands into a sea of green leaves and yellow flowers of the dubbeltjie, or "little devil", Tribulus terrestris. Named for its thorns – devilish for bare feet – it has a nutritive value comparable to that of lucerne.*

The dubbeltjie Tribulus terrestris covers the dunes after the first rains.

One of the chorus of millions, a barking gecko, not often
seen but always heard on summer evenings.

had no hope of reaching Nossob camp, a mere 70 km further north. The storm had split to move across my path and also cut me off from Twee Rivieren, driving me further and further to the east, into Botswana. So land I had to – thank goodness for an old disused strip graded years before next to the dry Nossob riverbed. Without any inspection flight of the potential landing site, I went straight in. The wide-eyed San sitting next to me went grey with fear. The whole of that day and night we had to sit and wait, and the most annoying thing of all was that it did not rain on us at all!

Flying above the rolling dunes, grassy flats and open dry tree savanna gives one the added advantage of seeing the Kalahari from another perspective. The greener circles, evidence of good rains, dot the landscape and vividly paint a patch-work picture of good and bad areas on the red background. Noting these temporary oases and their distribution in relation to the movement patterns of the large antelope improves one's understanding of this vast natural ecosystem.

During 1985/86, the worst two years in the last 10-year drought, these green patches were few and far between. All animals moved over larger ranges. Eland covered the greatest areas, ranging extensively over both Parks and beyond their boundaries. One adult cow I have been following for four years covered an area of 14 000 km² in those dry years. With gradual improvement in rain each year to 1988, so the green patches grew larger and more common; sometimes they joined to cover huge areas. This resulted in a radical reduction in the eland cow's ranging behaviour and her home range declined by almost 40% to 8 500 km². The same happened in the case of collared gemsbok, hartebeest, wildebeest and springbok whose ranges shrank from 1 420 km² to 560 km²; from 1 854 km² to 1 000 km²; from 3 616 km² to 300 km² and from 2 487 km² to 1 500 km² respectively.

The ranges of carnivores such as lions, leopards and hyaenas showed similar expansion and contraction, but to a much more limited extent. Their social organisation of prides and clans is very dependent upon claims to areas, so instead of simply expanding their territories to make up for prey animals being less common, their cubs began to die, with the result that the total numbers in the groups did not increase. When the situation became even more desperate, adults began to die and conflicts over the now very limited food supplies began to split and break up the groups.

Old and young male lions ejected from their prides wandered over huge distances, mostly on their own, or with their brothers or other wandering males they teamed up with. In one case an adolescent male lion I had marked was chased from his home pride near the confluence of the Auob and Nossob riverbeds by the resident male. This adolescent moved alone for about three months before dying 70 km into Botswana, unable to survive on his own. Two old males, no longer able to hold their prides, met the same fate at least 80 km from where they had originally been marked.

The vegetation in these green patches varies radically, depending on the amount of rain and spacing between rainstorms. Reasonable storms, well spaced, can encourage such luxuriant growth that the once completely naked sands with isolated trees can be turned into a parkland of tall, waving green grasses. The previously desolate fossil riverbeds and pans in no time push up bright green annuals and lush, nutritious grasses that the antelope greedily descend upon. Where the ephemerals can take hold first and smother out the young grass seedlings, the once uniformly red dunes or white riverbed sands are often transformed into a sea of brilliant yellow dubbeltjies *Tribulus terrestris*, interspersed with purple cat's tail *Herbstaedtia odorata* and "opslag" *Indigofera alternans*. The response to the rain is rapid: the three-thorned bushes *Rhigozum trichotomum* produce their white and pink flowers within five days and nutritious pods a week later. Speed is of the essence to make the best use of the available soil moisture while it lasts, before the hot sun draws it slowly to the surface to evaporate into the blue expanse above.

Research on wild animals often necessitates their capture for marking, attaching collars with radio-transmitters, searching for external parasites or collecting blood, but the animal should walk away unscathed and unstressed. The drug M99, administered through a syringe fired from a dart rifle, has revolutionised the capture of large wild mammals. The animal takes 5 to 10 minutes to become immobilised, but still needs careful handling, as a poor shot or low dosage does not fully anaesthetise the animal. Gemsbok in this state are particularly dangerous. Once the radio-collar is attached or samples collected an antidote M5050 is administered and the animal quickly recovers and runs off, just a little bewildered by the humans close by.

IX. ORYX CAPENSIS — THE GEMSBOK.

Dense stands of the sour smelling annual grass *Schmidtia kalahariensis* usually cover vast areas of the southern Kalahari after good rains. A pioneer, the first grass to recolonise barren disturbed areas after droughts or overgrazing, it will later make way for perennial grasses in the successional advancement of the different types of plants. This grass, good fodder when just sprouting or when dried out, is however highly unpalatable when ripe. It exudes an irritating substance that wets one's legs when walking through it and soon causes discomfort. The light grey-white colour of gemsbok's legs and faces soon becomes a dirty brown and they (at least the females) soon escape to the more open fossil riverbeds and pans to avoid any further contact with the grass. For cattle and sheep, this sour grass often causes eye in-

fections and swelling of the tongue. Farms usually covered in dense stands of it are avoided where possible. Its abundant growth often points to previously poor management practices.

Even in its dry state the sour grass is a problem, particularly for vehicles. Its prolific seed heads in no time clog up a vehicle radiator. One February I set off with two companions to retrieve a collar from a dead eland 200 km into Botswana. It was an incredibly hot day, reaching over 42° C in the vehicle cab. We had not gone more than 50 km when the engine's temperature gauge climbed well into the red. The radiator was completely blocked and useless as a cooler. It took us the next 12 hours and 60 ℓ of drinking water to cool the engine before reaching the next fresh water point in the Mabuasehube Game Reserve. After a further two days'

WHAT IS RADIO-TRACKING?

The fairly modern innovation of essentially a battery-powered miniature transmitter, generally attached to a collar harness or suitable protuberance (e.g. glued to a seal's head or bird's feather or drilled into a rhino horn), emits a pulsed signal via a broadcasting antenna. In the case of my collars, which consisted of hard, flexible plastic, the antenna was a whip of wire protruding from the collar, which fitted snugly around the animal's neck. The signal (generally of VHF of greater than 100 MHz) is inaudible to the subject and broadcasts a substantial distance, depending on the battery strength, position of the animal and the receiving station. Flying in the aircraft ZS-IYP, 1 200 m above ground, I can detect a collar up to 40 km away, but on the ground the distance drops to a mere 4 km.

Through an antenna and receiver on my end, the signal is transferred into an audible "beep" sound. Depending on the type of antenna used, the signal can indicate direction, as the signal volume becomes stronger or weaker depending on whether the receiving antenna is pointing at or away from the transmitter. This however gives no indication of distance, which can be determined by following the signal directly to the animal or by taking bearings from different localities and calculating the animal's "fix" through a method known as triangulation. Thus the important biological question, "Where is the animal?" can be answered fairly easily. In the southern Kalahari, my vast study area, locating only five animals from the ground by driving in a vehicle took me up to three days — not

search, we still had not found the collar. Now I always carry more water than fuel!

At the start of the rains, in its dried-out state, this sour grass is easily set alight by lightning. In late 1976, after excellent rains, the dense stands of sour grass were set ablaze by early lightning storms. For days the fires lit the evening sky. The Auob and Nossob riverbeds, previously effective fire-breaks with their shiny, naked surfaces, had become densely vegetated gardens, providing perfect crossing points for the roaring fires to jump between the Parks. Old, beautiful camel-thorn trees and dense grassy plains were completely destroyed. Terrible as it was, these fires are nature's way of controlling the build-up of moribund or dead standing vegetation in these arid areas after exceptional rains.

Only once this century, in 1934, has the Nossob flooded down its entire length to join the Molopo river. On the other hand, the Auob floods about once every 11 years. These floods bring not only the welcome water but also flooded roads, and malaria. Malaria outbreaks in 1934 killed the first park warden and many members of the local farming community. As recently as 1988, even with average rains, people still died of the disease when the Kuruman and Auob rivers flooded, cutting off the Parks for at least three weeks.

Once the rare floods recede or the scattered storms pass, the isolated pools or kolks of water in the riverbeds and pans gradually become collection points for birds, antelope (wildebeest mostly), insects and man. During the German campaign against the Hottentot rebels in 1904, most of these kolks were guarded by German garrisons in an attempt to deny the Hottentots drinking water. They drank tsamma juices instead, which are often sweeter than the muddy kolk waters. Geinab, now known as Grootkolk, in the Kalahari Gemsbok National Park was one of these outposts on the dry Nossob riverbed. It was far from anywhere and hardly anybody knew or cared about it. But for Simon Kooper, one of the Hottentot leaders, it was the place of a great victory. An early-morning surprise attack by his band completely routed the German soldiers. The few that survived the initial attack were stripped of their clothes and shot in the back as they marched away, in retaliation for the ruthless tactics the Germans used. Old tins stamped with German words, empty cartridge cases and ammunition clips are still to be found littering the sands at the now famous kolk.

No sooner have the first pools filled than the dragonflies in their hundreds begin to mate and perform acrobatic flights while laying their eggs in the shallow pools. Most of these pools are ephemeral, lasting from a few hours to some days, but a few, sparsely scattered along the Nossob river, last for months. As dragonfly larvae are restricted to life under water for a year or more, it has often intrigued me where all the adults come from

particularly cost-effective. From the air the method of location is similar. While flying I set both my antennae (which are fixed to the struts on each side of the aircraft) to listen for incoming signals. On receiving a signal through the receiver and my earphone, I switch from both antennae to each one separately to determine which is receiving the stronger signal. If, for instance, the left-hand antenna has the loudest signal I then

turn to the right, raising the receiving antenna higher and so improving the reception, and do a full circle watching my compass constantly for the direction of the loudest bleep. On descending to tree-top level I visually locate the animal, noting the group size, body condition, presence/absence of a calf and habitat, as well as of course the position as determined from bearings and flying time from known features around.

in early summer. A few species are migratory, but the majority probably breed in the artificial waterholes scattered in the South African park and surrounding farms.

As it becomes progressively drier between rainstorms, the water dependent and granivorous Cape turtle *Streptopelia capicola* and Namaqua doves *Oena capensis* teem in their hundreds to these kolks to drink. Pairs of lanner falcons *Falco biarmicus* resident around waterholes also swoop down in dozens to drink water and hunt. The doves' only protection is their overwhelming numbers and the confusion thus created. To early travellers in the southern Kalahari the morning cooing of the doves was always welcome, as it meant drinking water nearby.

Namaqua sandgrouse *Pterocles namaqua* and Burchell's sandgrouse *P. burchelli* fly in from up to 60 km away, arriving mid-morning at the waterhole. Descending almost vertically to the water's edge after circling overhead a few times, they drink quickly and fly away. The breeding males wade into the water and dunk their breast and lower abdomen feathers. These feathers, and particularly the barbules that make up the vane of the feather, show peculiar modifications. Instead of being straight as in the typical feather, the barbules at their base are helically coiled when dry. On being wetted, they uncoil and stand at right angles to the feather vane, forming a dense mat in which drinking

water for the chicks is trapped. The sandgrouse's poor kidney development, limited ability to concentrate their urine, lack of salt glands and granivorous diet make them dependent upon drinking water. Therefore, like the doves and other seed-eating birds, they are highly nomadic, always in search of water and suitable food sources. But like the dragonflies they have also become permanent residents in the southern Kalahari owing to the scattered permanent water points for cattle and game.

From within the still, more permanent pools come the "brrruup" call of the African bull-frog, *Pyxicephalus adspersus*. Having emerged from their hidden burrows deep in the river clay from the previous summer or even the summer before that, they go about mating and feeding, before the pool dries up. To survive the dry winter months, they shut down their metabolism, using stored fat and protein for energy, and conserve water by storing all urine in an enlarged bladder from which water is actively reabsorbed back into the body. Using similar means to overwinter, Cape terrapins *Pelomedusa subrufa* also breed and feed in these scattered fresh rainwater pools.

The summer and the coming of rains herald not only a rebirth of the vegetation, but also a rejuvenation of most animal populations, from insects to the large antelope. The wildebeest generally drop their calves over a period of a month, starting in December

Several sweeps over the active collar without seeing the animal always makes me suspect that the animal is dead. On one occasion this happened with an eland cow I was looking for. Low passes next to the small pan soon revealed no eland but several small stick-and-grass shelters typically used by San and Kgalagadis.

A two-day journey by vehicle a week later introduced me to the world of poachers.

Lying around the then deserted camp were bones, pegging sticks for drying skins, old dried meat or biltong, discarded pelts and working utensils. My eland collar I located 30 m away, buried half a metre in the sand, the place cleverly marked with a stick. For the remainder of that day Hermanus and I tracked the departed poachers and their donkeys and horses but lost the spoor on a pan further to the west.

or later and continuing till February every year. Springbok tend to be less seasonal but still show peaks in the numbers of lambs dropped. These coordinated lambing times result from different environmental cues that set off the mating drive of active bulls and rams, and/or cause females to come into heat. The cues vary depending upon the species concerned and normally occur months before. For some species, such as wildebeest, the primary stimulation is a change in photoperiod or day length, while in others, such as many desert birds, the mere sight of rain is enough.

The advantage to wildebeest of dropping their calves simultaneously is analogous to doves drinking at waterholes in large numbers. The carnivores are swamped by newborn helpless young; only a relatively small number can be caught. A wildebeest or springbok newborn walks within 30 minutes and can run soon afterwards with the herd. Other less seasonal breeders such as gemsbok and red hartebeest rely on hiding their cryptically coloured calves alone for a few weeks until they are strong enough to run alongside the adults.

Among the insects, the hot weather and fluctuating moist and dry conditions result in swarms of different species streaming from the sands and trees. Large yellow African migrant butterflies *Catopsilia florella*, then African monarchs *Danaus chrysippus* and painted ladies *Cynthia* spp., different species of stinkbugs and armoured ground crickets follow in succession during the day. At night, the same occurs with many different species of moths and dung beetles fluttering around the Kalahari sands. Capitalising on these insect and rodent booms, several migrant birds move into the Kalahari. Large concentrations of Abdim's storks *Ciconia abdimii* and a few interspersed white storks *C. ciconia* grace the riverbeds and pans in their search for caterpillars, grasshoppers and other insects. Kurrichane buttonquails *Turnix sylvatica* and harlequin quails *Coturnix delegorguei* similarly move into the dense riverbed undergrowth after good rains in their search for seeds.

Predatory birds such as yellowbilled kites *Milvus migrans* from the Middle East and Europe, steppe buzzards *Buteo buteo* from central Asia and the odd Wahlberg's eagle *Aquila wahlbergi* from tropical Africa, to name a few, pass through on their yearly migration.

Carnivorous insects such as the oogpister beetle (or eye squirter) *Anthia* spp., active day and night, comb the sands for other insects and dead animal matter. This ferocious beetle has an efficient means of defence. It can squirt a fine jet of a hot, pungent, organic acid solution when disturbed and is known to cause blindness in cats and chickens, hence the colloquial name. Eric Pianka, a famous herpetologist, has suggested that the stilt walking, or stiff-legged and arched-back behaviour of the vividly coloured black and yellow juvenile Kalahari sand lizard *Eremias lugubris*, in fact mimics *Anthia* to warn would-be predators away.

The dung beetle fulfils a highly important role in the Kalahari and in the rest of Africa, India, Southeast Asia and of late Australia. Their habit of removing dung and burying it, with their brood of eggs inside, controls the spread of disease, flies, internal parasites and bacteria as well as fertilises the soil and facilitates the spread and germination of the many plant seeds in the dung. The dung beetle's effectiveness is highly dependent upon ideal weather conditions during the summer months. I have noticed that on warm, moist days gemsbok and wildebeest dung is completely buried within half an hour. This has proven very frustrating for me when trying to collect faecal samples for analysis because it meant that samples had to be collected the moment they had been deposited by the animal, before the dung beetles got to work! However, during the winter months when the dung beetles are not active, faeces clutter the sand surfaces in places and their nutrients are potentially lost to the system.

With the first summer rains, hordes of winged termites or alates of both sexes emerge from the deep caverns of the underground termitaria. This occur-

On another occasion I found one of my collared lions dead just outside the Park boundary. Landing at Twee Rivieren, Elias le Riche and I immediately drove to retrieve the collar. We found that the plastic strapping of the collar had been cut through with a knife. An inspection of the area revealed deep but fairly old vehicle tracks. We followed them, using San trackers, who showed us where the poachers had

chased the male, then shot him while he crouched behind a bush.

Hard, caked blood was still evident. There was nothing we could do, as the now long-gone poachers would just claim that the lion had harassed their stock. They now had a good skin with which to make a lot of money, but hopefully it would be their last, as word would soon get around that we know about their activities.

rence, even though sporadic, is rapidly capitalised upon by the many predators of termites: lizards, rodents, birds of prey, mongooses, jackals, foxes, aardvark and sometimes humans. However, throughout the year, termites form the basis of a huge food chain, upon which several species are totally dependent, such as the aardwolf and the aardvark or antbear.

Even though not immediately obvious, the silent impact made by termites is impressive. In arid regions, with the different species foraging at different times and places, they can alone consume up to 25% of the vegetation. They carry predominantly dead, dry, coarse and useless grasses and sticks deep into their termitaria. There, under controlled temperatures and humidity, *Trinervitermes* spp. and *Hodotermes mossambicus* partially digest the grasses and feed them to each other for food. Thus the dead grass material, useless to the ungulates, is converted into a readily available food source in the form of termites for a wide range of animals to utilise throughout the year.

And so the rainstorms, sporadic in time and distribution, create a mosaic of boom areas surrounded by regions where life stands still. As these small oases begin to recede, having received no follow-up rain, so other areas flourish, creating a dynamic system that varies from place to place on an apparently dull, monotonous red Kalahari sand background. This is summer, the time of excitement, rebirth and frustration.

Territorial wildebeest bulls space themselves along the Nossob and Auob riverbeds waiting for the roaming female herds. They roll in their dung piles to advertise to other wildebeest bulls who exactly the territory's owner is.

(Overleaf) *Johan, Kalahari boy, with his pet meerkat.*

133

THE TIME
OF BITTER
COLD

Summer rains bring newborns to the Kalahari.

The days grow shorter, the nights longer. The leaves of the black-thorn *Acacia* begin to shrivel and gently fall to the red sand. Green grass slowly fades to a soft yellow-golden blanket over the rolling dunes as the months march on and April becomes May. Then the cold strikes, cutting and slicing its way up the riverbeds, along the dune streets, through every bush and tree and into every nook and cranny. Some nights the freezing south wind plummets the mercury to at least -7° C – this is the other formidable face of the Kalahari. Roaring camp fires and hot sleeping-bags do little to contain the biting cold. Fortunately, such extremely cold nights are not common: the average minimum for the winter months is around 2° C.

Arid regions characteristically have cold winters, owing to little ground cover to prevent the radiation of heat back into the open night skies. The normally low humidities also facilitate the loss of heat from the ground, thus exposing animal and plant life to the other extreme of arid environments – cold stress, just as dangerous as excessive heat.

Most ectothermic animals (relying upon the sun as an external heat source to warm their bodies), such as the insects and lizards, escape the cold by burrowing beneath the sand or into holes in tree trunks, or over-winter through hibernation or in the form of larvae and eggs. Reptiles such as the puff-adder, yellow cobra and rare large likkewaan or monitor lizard *Varanus exanthematicus* hibernate in hidden burrows, using their stored fat reserves to keep their metabolism ticking over. Scorpions similarly escape into their burrows during very cold weather before emerging to move majestically over the sand with weapons drawn – pincers forward and stinging tail held curled and ready overhead for any soft-fleshed insect to feed upon. Being adapted to the cooler noc-

Sociable weavers often build their huge communal nests in dry trees. This enables them to see approaching predators easily and makes access more difficult for the Cape cobra, which seizes many chicks.

turnal period they can operate with relatively low body temperatures and it is assumed that their whole physiology is adapted for this.

The lizards show some intriguing behavioural variations owing to their different colours and preferred habitats. The ability of the black, arboreal skinks *Mabua* spp. to absorb more heat faster, owing to their colour and habit of perching high in the trees where they receive early morning and late afternoon sun, allows them to be active when ambient temperatures are low and their terrestrial counterparts are snugly hiding within their burrows. Moreover, these same trees provide a well-shaded environment during the midday heat, permitting the skinks to remain active during that period. The ground dwelling sand lizards, living in an environment with overall lower plant cover, a later sunrise and earlier sunset and less shade during midday, experience a more difficult thermal environment. Their light colours and hence greater reflectivity and fast locomotion allow them to remain active longer in their more exposed habitats. During winter they can remain active throughout the day, but in summer their activity is restricted to the early mornings and late afternoons. Interestingly, the activity of one of their main predators, the pygmy falcon, correlates exactly with that of the sand lizards.

A whole different set of physiological principles governs the endothermic animals (animals that generate their own heat from within), such as mammals and birds. Their main aim is to try to maintain a constant body temperature of around 37° C at all times whether environmental temperatures are cold or hot. However, the insulation properties – thickness and physical quality – of desert mammals' fur are essentially designed for coping with high environmental temperatures and not with cold. Their hides' colour, thickness and quality are principally designed for shielding out the sun's energy and getting rid of excessive body heat, as is well illustrated in the light grey and brown pelts of gemsbok and springbok. Even the short, light brown, glossy coats of the local Afrikaner cattle, extensively farmed in the Kala-

The humble abode of a Kalahari farmer and his family in the early days.

hari, are ideally suited for reflecting the sun's energy – better than the long woolly coats of certain British breeds.

So when the cold weather strikes, mammals of different shapes and sizes attempt to cope in several different ways. As for reptiles and insects, escape is an important strategy, particularly for those small enough to use burrows. Some rodents, such as the pouched mouse, resort to torpor to save energy. However, as most of the Kalahari's small mammals are nocturnally active and must feed, they attempt to change their activity patterns from those of summer to avoid being above ground for too long when it is intensely cold. This the pouched mouse does by feeding upon stored food items underground in the safety of the burrow. In much the same way, we humans escape into the warmth of our insulated houses and do not emerge until after sunrise.

Nevertheless, being active in cold weather requires the expenditure of considerable amounts of energy to maintain body temperature, and as energy and water are both usually limited in arid environments and consequently do not allow for much deposition of fat reserves, this means that the animals often walk on an energy tightrope. After prolonged droughts, severe cold can be fatal for many animals, which may partly account for the high mortality of wildebeest and eland in poor condition during the winter of 1985.

The aardwolf *Proteles cristatus*, a specialist termite feeder, experiences extreme stress during the cold winter months. During this period it loses up to 20% of its body mass, and cub mortalities are greatest. This results from the fact that aardwolfs eat almost entirely *Trinervitermes* termites. During the cold winter months these termites' above-ground activity is greatly reduced, and owing to the aardwolf's specially adapted mouth, it cannot change to eating other insects. So the aardwolf seeks out in compensation the more diurnal harvester termites *Hodotermes*, but these appear infrequently.

At temperatures below 10° C, aardwolfs abandon foraging and escape into burrows, where it is suggested they also go into a state of torpor in order to reduce

(Inset overleaf) A San woman "exhibited" in Europe.

(Below) "It was comfortable and served its purpose" say Theunis and Truia in front of their first home on their Kalahari sheep farm.

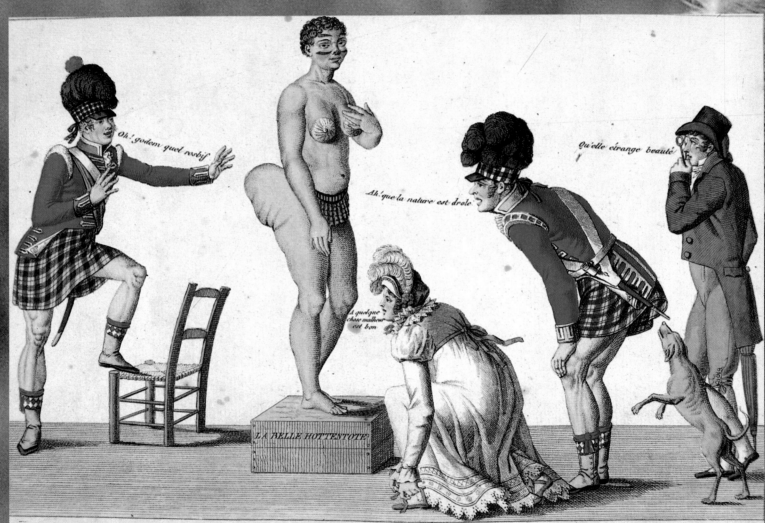

Les Curieux en extase,
ou les Cordons de souliers.

OUR FRIENDS THE HYAENAS

Portrayed as a devious scavenger pestering beautiful lions and leopard, and robbing camps of their rubbish in the still of the night, the spotted hyaena is not popular.

Gus Mills, researcher for 13 years in the Kalahari Gemsbok National Park, ably introduced me to other aspects of this highly intelligent and interesting carnivore. Over the last 11 years, the behaviour of the Kousaunt clan in the Kalahari Gemsbok National Park has been closely monitored and we have both witnessed the intimate goings-on in a very close family unit, through birth and death, feast and famine.

Each individual has its own character which we have grown to love and respect in this harsh environment. Olivia, the matriarch and boss of the clan from 1978 until recently when she died of rabies, was the epitome of strength and confidence, calling the tune in every decision. Goldie, her daughter and successor, follows Olivia's example. Hans, who also tragically died of rabies, has been succeeded by Graham; both played the typical role of the shy, excluded male. But when it comes to hunting and killing for the clan they are in the forefront — and fearless. In every clan there is generally only one breeding male, a highly sought after position by every young male. Males

are chased from their home clans once they become reproductively active. For the male, the clan means security and a regular meal and, most important of all, it provides breeding opportunities. Alone and ostracised, males are exposed to the harsh realities of the Kalahari. In trying to gain access to a clan, beating the resident male is not enough: they must be acceptable to the adult females who want the best mates to father their offspring.

The close bonds, relationships and dominance in the clan are maintained through intricate greeting ceremonies that entail many groans and whines and profuse sniffing and licking of the enlarged reproductive organs of both sexes. Such greetings occur around the communal dens where the breeding females leave their cubs, after moments of drama such as fights with other clans or carni-

vores, at latrines or just while foraging.

However, even within the clan there are strong allegiances, and these occur between mother and close kin. This phenomenon, known in biological jargon as "kin selection", is the central theme in all advanced animal communities and helps explain most of their social behaviour. It is based on the idea that by helping your close kin or blood relatives to survive and breed, you are in fact also promoting the spread of your own genes or genetic material, thus ensuring its survival in the population. Goldie one night while out foraging illustrated this beautifully. Members of the clan had killed a subadult springbok, which supplies enough meat for three adult hyaenas at the most. Goldie, being the matriarch, aggressively snatched the carcass from two other females (her

cousins), denying them access while she and her two cubs, Lorna and Rian, fed.

When the Kousaunt clan grew too large for its territory and its food supply, the clan split — rather aggressively. In fact the clan divided right down family lines with Olivia and Goldie and their sons and daughters remaining, while Two-Two (probably Olivia's sister) and her progeny left. In the meantime a further split has occurred in the Olivia-Goldie alliance, demonstrating the force of kin selection in spotted hyaenas.

Owing to the dry, generally waterless conditions of the southern Kalahari, the spotted hyaenas kill more live prey than other populations in wetter parts of Africa. This is essentially their only source of water, unlike the brown hyaenas who scavenge more and hence rely upon melons for water.

The southern Kalahari differs from the central Kalahari in having a fairly large resident spotted hyaena population. Why should this be, as the southern Kalahari is drier and hence has lower productivity and game numbers? I think the two large dry riverbeds, the Auob and Nossob, and their associated better quality vegetation and important mineral licks and, of late, permanent water supplies are a stabilising factor to large numbers of springbok, gemsbok and wildebeest, thus enabling spotted hyaena clans to stabilise. On the other hand, the central Kalahari with its less common riverine and pan habitats and more nomadic and fluctuating game populations probably does not allow the establishment of fairly fixed spotted hyaena clans.

energy loss. The fairly formidable looking long fur of the aardwolf probably has dual functions: to make the animal look larger, but also to provide a warm coat that allows it to forage longer on cool nights. Brown hyaenas are similarly equipped with long coats that probably enable them to penetrate into the cold, windy and exposed Namib coast in search of seal carcasses. By contrast the spotted hyaenas with their shorter coats remain 20 km inland from the coast.

The aardwolf is one of the few mammals that feed on *Trinervitermes* in spite of the termites' highly effective chemical defence system, which consists of a sticky and noxious secretion produced by the soldiers. The aardwolf's gut is particularly resistant to these chemicals, which are readily excreted in the faeces. This probably accounts for the fact that nothing grows on aardwolf latrine sites, which can be clearly seen among the dense stands of sour grass after good rains. As aardwolfs rely greatly upon their

sense of smell to locate foraging termites, they bury their faeces so that no confusion can arise.

Bat-eared foxes *Otocyon megalotis*, also insect eaters, are more versatile than aardwolfs. Restricted to foraging predominantly at night in the hot summer, they shift to foraging in the early morning and late afternoon in winter, thus escaping the cold. Also, they do not concentrate only on termites, but feed on a wide array of insects and their larvae, which they detect below the sand with their highly sensitive and expressive ears. On hearing a grub, with rapid little digs they excavate their prize and consume it before moving on in a jerky manner.

Ratels or honey badgers *Mellivora capensis* forage later into the cool winter mornings in search of active lizards and mice. Realising the advantage of following the ratel, one, and sometimes up to three, pale chanting goshawks eagerly fly in tow from perch to perch, in the hope of grabbing an escaping rodent scared by the honey badger. I have seen honey bad-

The sniffing and licking of each other's genitals form an important part of the greeting ceremony of spotted hyaenas, which probably facilitates the maintenance of social bonds between individuals. Generally the subordinate individual raises its leg first and sometimes bares its teeth and flattens its ears as part of appeasing the dominant individual.

(Preceding pages) *Spotted hyaenas change dens roughly once every month because of a build-up of the flea population living in the sands of the den, usually a deserted antbear or porcupine hole. When the adults leave to hunt in their huge 1 200 km² territory, the hyaena cubs remain in the security of the den. The cubs rely entirely upon their own mothers' milk for well over a year before joining in the hunt.*

gers digging eagerly into rodent burrows, then suddenly stop and bang their hind feet loudly on the ground in the hope of scaring out the mice, while goshawks hop around the other side of the burrow system in anticipation of an easy meal. The honey badgers do not take too kindly to the goshawks' behaviour and will jump at them if they approach too closely – besides, now and then an adult goshawk would make an excellent meal!

Desert mammals of less than 4 kg have another method of coping with the cold. They resort to a mechanism known as non-shivering thermogenesis, which is the act of burning a specific type of high energy brown fat, stored in certain places in the animal's body. This adaptation varies seasonally, but occurs widely among the rodent community. In the striped mouse, the most common diurnally active rodent in the southern Kalahari, it has been found that decreasing day length after summer initiates the rodent's ability to utilise this fat and may also influence its storage in preparation of winter.

(Page 152) The mounds of snouted or Trinervitermes termites are frequently found on the flat plain along the Nossob riverbed. Besides being the home or hive of the termites, they also make ideal vantage points for jackals and meerkats.

(Page 153) The scarce martial eagle, king of raptors in the Kalahari. Pairs are spaced at 10 km to 15 km intervals along the riverbeds where suitable breeding sites are available. They hunt for hares, meerkats, mongooses and even springbok and steenbok lambs. In the adjacent sheep farming areas they are unjustly shot for killing the odd sheep lamb.

The small whitefaced owl eyes the Kalahari night.

Animals above 4 kg, like the Cape and bat-eared foxes and black-backed jackals, attempt to improve the quality and thickness of their fur coats in winter to reduce the loss of body heat. It is then that they are intensively hunted for their beautiful pelts to make karosses. As body size increases so fur thickness generally declines because the need to reradiate or lose excess body heat becomes important, particularly on hot days or after a hard long chase.

In addition all these animals, up to the size of gemsbok and eland, resort to energetically expensive muscle shivering as an extra source of heat on cold days. Other behavioural means such as huddling together, lying down and covering up exposed body areas, and even just sheltering away from cold winds, help in energy and heat conservation.

Anette, my wife and companion, has been long intrigued by the reasons why animals group together. Ground squirrels, on which her research activities have been centred, have revealed some interesting facts about huddling. When exposed to cold tempera-

tures of 14° C, the difference in the amount of energy saved between two or six squirrels huddled together can be up to 40%. Huddling as a means to share each other's warmth and survive the cold nights is practised by the vast majority of rodents, birds such as small pygmy falcons, through to jackals, springbok and wildebeest.

For many of the resident large birds of prey, winter is the time to breed. Lappetfaced, whitebacked and a few whiteheaded vultures; tawny and martial eagles; pale chanting goshawks and lanner falcons make their nests atop the large camel-thorn trees, catching the sun's welcome winter warmth as they incubate their eggs and protect their young chicks from the elements. Their large body size allows them to resist the cold nights much better than their smaller counterparts, such as the blacksshouldered kites, gabar goshawks, rednecked falcons, pygmy falcons, whitefaced owls and pearlspotted owls, which restrict their breeding to the warmer spring months. Even though the small pearlspotted owl and pygmy

A choking blanket of dust brings darkness to the dead riverbed.

(Opposite) *Rippled sand dunes permanently thrown into long lines by the prevailing strong north wind.*

A Cape Mounted Police patrol.

(Overleaf) *During the worst drought of the decade, in 1985, thousands of carcasses such as this one were lying scattered along the dirt road.*

falcon use well insulated woodpecker holes and sociable weaver nests to breed in, thus efficiently escaping the rigours of the outside Kalahari environment, their small bodies and associated high metabolism cannot resist cold exposure for long.

The first frost of winter kills the annual grasses and causes the perennial grasses to withdraw their nutrients into their protected root systems. Thus the once green stands of grass become almost completely yellow and much poorer in quality. It is then that the antelope, small and large, begin to feel the pinch of winter. Their different abilities to pick out good leaves and flowers from here and there, begin to count towards their surviving until the first rains. Wildebeest, unable to select individual leaves, begin to move to water or areas containing tsamma melons. Eland begin to move westward, towards the dune country of the southern Kalahari, for its important evergreen grey camel-thorn *Acacia*, shepherd's tree and sometimes good crops of nutritious annuals that paint the dunes with colour. Gemsbok, springbok and steenbok stay more or less in their normal ranges, as their small, nimble mouths and supple lips allow them to pick and choose.

With the cold comes also the modern-day hunter or tourist to capture the magic of the Kalahari. It is in fact on them that this last natural wilderness in the southern Kalahari depends. With almost the whole of the South African and the entire Namibian southern Kalahari divided up into farms, and with only one reserve, the Kalahari Gemsbok National Park, the initiative lies with Botswana.

However, because of the excellent incentives offered by the EEC over the last 20 years for Botswanan beef, much more money has been invested in the cattle industry and the national herd has increased from 1,2 million in 1966 to nearly 4 million head of cattle in 1984/85. But the emphasis has been on increasing numbers rather than improving the quality of the herds. To sustain this vast herd, boreholes have been sunk further into the central and southern Kahalari. Unfortunately, good ranch management practices have not followed this advance; the old traditional methods of communal, shared lands remain. This encourages rapid degradation of the veld around the waterholes and stimulates further moves to better grazing elsewhere, where the cycle is repeated. Throughout this whole process wildlife has had to give way. Traditionally, game has provided for up to 60% of the meat consumed in Botswana, but this has declined in the face of the expanding cattle industry. As the cattle are principally owned by only a few people, the vast majority of underprivileged people who relied on game as a source of food have now begun to suffer.

Fortunately, realising the potential of game, the Botswana government developed a Wildlife Conservation Policy to stop the decline of their valuable heritage. Wildlife have the advantage of being adapted to the Kalahari better than the introduced cattle. So for relatively little effort the economic returns in the form of trophy money, hunters' licences, meat, skins and tourism can be of the order of more than 17 times the expenditure. Recently, Wildlife Management Areas where exploitation of wildlife in all its forms can take place, have been created throughout Botswana. Some surround the Botswana Gemsbok National park, thus providing a necessary buffer zone between undisturbed sanctuaries and cattle ranching areas in the southern Kalahari.

In South Africa and Namibia the wildlife industry has gone a step further with the development of game farm enterprises in conjunction with normal sheep and cattle farming. In this way a greater range of herbivores with different feeding habits account for better veld utilisation than just cattle and sheep alone. But the populations have to be closely monitored to prevent overgrazing in a system essentially suited to a nomadic style of utilisation, which was the case prior to the erection of fences.

With the potential for game fully realised within the constraints of a burgeoning human population, the future of the southern Kalahari must be approached with sound forethought, imagination and caution, as any errors now made may well be irreversible. For the sake of those free-living populations, remnants of the once great Kalahari herds, the single most important factor is space in which to roam, escape and bloom, in order to survive the rigours of the dust, rain and cold of the southern Kalahari.

A German police station along the northern border.

ACKNOWLEDGEMENTS:

Theunis and Truia Botha
Dennis Da Silva
Rion De Klerk
Marty De Kock
Gunther Dettweiller
Ken and Priscilla Eva
Dr. M. Greenberg
Michel and Françoise Guignard
Al and Ann Hansel
Danie Hough
Michael and Lisa Kloeckner
John and Gina Kramer
Derek and Rosemary Krause
Elias and Doempie Le Riche
Klaus D. Matzke

The Meano brothers
George and Shane Mennie
Andre and Anna Moolman
Jennis Mullan
Japie Naudé
Rudolph Nortier
Karin Olivier
Charl Steyn
Eric and Mariana Steyn
Johan and Rita Van Dyk
Theard Van Heerden
Eric and Karen Walker
Ann Wanless
Lt-Col. Weise
Heather Wildi

THE AFRICANA MUSEUM
BEITH PROCESS
CABLE SERVICES
EASIGAS
THE NATIONAL PARKS BOARD
THE OFFICE OF THE PRESIDENT AND WILDLIFE
DEPARTMENT OF BOTSWANA
SAFRIC
SATOUR
STE BRICE ROBERT
SOUTH AFRICAN AIRWAYS
THE UPINGTON MUSEUM

Photographs on page 33 (bottom right) and page 117 (bottom right) : Jacques GONTARD
Photograph on page 112: Fred STOLPER